Presented By
The American Bar Association
Young Lawyers Division and the
ABA-CLE Career Resource Center

A Lawyer's Guide to Networking

**By
Susan R. Sneider, J.D.**

**Defending Liberty
Pursuing Justice**

Cover graphic illustration courtesy of Ethan Leland.

The materials contained herein represent the opinions of the authors and editors and should not be construed to be the action of the American Bar Association Young Lawyers Division or the ABA-CLE Career Resource Center unless adopted pursuant to the bylaws of the Association.

Nothing contained in this book is to be considered as the rendering of legal advice for specific cases, and readers are responsible for obtaining such advice from their own legal counsel. This book and any forms and agreements herein are intended for educational and informational purposes only.

ISBN: 1-59031-732-7; 978-1-59031-732-7
Product Code: CEV06LGNB

To: The Honorable Seymour F. Simon,
my first professional mentor

Table of Contents

Chapter Eight: Networking for Business Development 91

Chapter Nine: Networking for Your Next Job 99

Chapter Ten: Follow-Up and Databases 119

A Final Thought 129

About the Author 131

Acknowledgments

I come from a tradition of giving back. My mother and father graduated from medical school together in 1938. Growing up I remember all the neighborhood kids squirming in our kitchen while getting bandaged and splintered from their mishaps. No one was ever billed—it was just part of being a friend and a neighbor. For years, my parents ran the charity ball for their hospital; I remember the hours they spent planning the event and negotiating the table seating. Thus started my networking training—the notion of both connecting with everyone in our community and giving back to one's family, friends, neighbors and colleagues.

There have been so many wonderful people in my life who have taught me about how the world works when you are open and giving that it would fill all the pages of this book to name them. So, from the bottom of my heart, I thank each and every one of you and only regret that I cannot acknowledge everyone individually.

Three extraordinary networkers—Pamela Rose, President, Rose & Associates (Chicago-based tenant representation firm); Gary Pines, Harding & Associates (rainmaking coach); and Steve Warshal, Centaur Conferences (London-based international conference organizer)—deserve special recognition. All rekindled in me a love for networking and an appreciation for how networking provides opportunities for others.

I also wish to thank two incredibly connected people in the legal industry—Kathy Morris, Chief Career Development Officer at Gardner Carton & Douglas LLP, and Jill Eckert McCall, Director, ABA Young Lawyers Division—who graciously allowed me to use portions of their networking materials. Thanks also to my two dedicated readers, Elliot Molk, partner at Barack Ferrazzano Kirschbaum Perlman &

Nagelberg LLP, and Toni E. Lesowitz, Ph.D, President of The Lesowitz Group, Inc. (organizational design and development).

A heartfelt "thank you" to all of those who gave of their time and spirit to be interviewed.

Friends are life's special gifts. Two deserve particular thanks: Sandy Brown, who, together with her Siberian Husky and my English Springer Spaniel, walks with me daily to and from the dog beach in sun, rain, mud and snow, talking about connecting and connections. And Marsha Sullivan, who kept me committed to the project with her constant e-mails and phone calls ("How many pages have you written now?"); her loving and nagging support were essential to the writing of this book.

I have been blessed with a wonderful husband, Jon Mills (my talented editor), and three spectacular daughters, Kimberly (a born networker), Jessica (whose relentless insistence that I write this book served as my muse), and Samantha (a gifted artist). I dedicate this book to the Mills clan with deep appreciation and love. They have endured years of their wife and mother saying, "No, it's not time to go yet, I still need to introduce ..."

Introduction and Instructions

This is a workbook. Bend pages you want to refer to, rip out pages you want to work with, and for goodness sakes, ignore the pages that are not useful to you.

Inside you will find advice and insight from some of the great networkers in the legal industry. I am extremely fortunate that these talented and successful individuals have graciously allowed me to share their stories and tips with you. Some of the quoted interviewees are dear old friends. Others came to me through warm introductions: referrals from mutual friends. Yet others were kind enough to take a call from a stranger in order to help out on a project about networking. They are all listed in the Roster immediately following this introduction. When you read their quotes, you may find it useful to return to the Roster to learn about their positions and backgrounds to better appreciate their perspectives and advice.

Here is my personal request: if you have made a useful net-working contact as a result of reading this book, please tell me your experience (contact me via the publisher) and let us know if we can tell your story to future audiences.

Roster of Quoted Networkers

Jonathan Asperger, Principal, Asperger Partners; former Director of Marketing and Communications, Mayer, Brown, Rowe & Maw LLP

Stephen Ball, Chief Executive Officer, Mourant du Feu & Juene (*The Lawyer* 2005 Offshore Firm of the Year); former Managing Director and International General Counsel, Kroll Inc.

Ray Bayley, Principal, Novus Law LLC

Debbie Berman, Partner, Jenner & Block LLP, *Crain's Chicago Business* 2005 "40 under 40"

N. Cornell Boggs, III, Chief Legal Officer and Group Vice President for Public Affairs, Coors Brewing Co.

David Brown, Chair, Management Committee, Much Shelist Freed Denenberg Ament & Rubenstein, P.C.

Kara Cenar, Partner, Bell, Boyd & Lloyd LLC; Chicago Chapter President, National Association of Women Business Owners (NAWBO)

Carolyn H. Clift, Vice-President, General Counsel & Assistant Secretary, Health Care Service Corporation (a Mutual Legal Reserve Company operating through its Divisions, Blue Cross and Blue Shield of Illinois, Texas, New Mexico, and Oklahoma)

Miriam J. Frank, Global Practice Leader In-House Placement, Major, Lindsey & Africa, LLC

John Garvey, Dean, Boston College School of Law

The Honorable Judge Joan B. Gottschall, United States District Court, Northern District of Illinois

John P. "Jack" Heinz, Owen L. Coon Professor of Law, Northwestern University School of Law; former Executive Director, American Bar Foundation

The Honorable Judge Michael B. Hyman, Circuit Court of Cook County, Illinois; former President, Chicago Bar Association

Allan J. Katz, Managing Shareholder, Akerman Senterfitt LLP

W. H. ("Joe") Knight, Jr., Dean, University of Washington Law School

Faye Knowles, Shareholder, Fredrikson & Byron, P.A.; former President, American Board of Certification (the only national certifying agency for bankruptcy and debtor-creditor attorneys)

Joan Lebow, Founder, Lebow & Malecki, LLC; former General Counsel, Illinois Masonic Medical Center

Francesca Maher, Chief Executive Officer, American Red Cross of Greater Chicago; former Senior Vice President and General Counsel, UAL Corporation and United Airlines

Lee Miller, Joint Chief Executive Officer, DLA Piper Rudnick Gray Cary (*The Lawyer* 2006 Global Law Firm of the Year)

John E. Mitchell, Principal, WomenCentric™ Enterprises

Michael A. Nemeroff, President, Vedder, Price, Kaufman & Krammholz, P.C.

Marla Persky, Vice President, General Counsel and Corporate Secretary, Boehringer Ingelheim Corporation

Gary Pines, Rainmaking Coach, Harding & Company

Debra E. Pole, Partner, Sidley Austin LLP

Nancy Rapoport, Professor and former Dean, University of Houston Law Center

Veta Richardson, Executive Director, Minority Corporate Counsel Association

Anna Richo, Vice President Law, Amgen Inc.

Manuel "Manny" Sanchez, Managing Partner, Sanchez Daniels & Hoffman LLP

Stephanie A. Scharf, Ph.D., Partner, Jenner & Block LLP; former President, National Association of Women Lawyers (NAWL)

Jerold Solovy, Chairman, Jenner & Block LLP

Nina Stillman, Partner, Morgan, Lewis & Bockius LLP

Sharan Ilene Tash, Founder/CEO, The Professional Networker, Inc.

Howard Tullman, President, Kendall College; Chairman of the Board, The Cobalt Group; Director, The Princeton Review

Brian Uzzi, Professor, Kellogg School of Management, Northwestern University

David E. Van Zandt, Dean and Professor of Law, Northwestern University School of Law

Jill Wine-Banks, Chief Officer, Education to Careers for the Chicago Public Schools; former Executive Vice-President and Chief Operating Officer, American Bar Association; former General Counsel, Department of the Army; former Assistant Watergate Special Prosecutor, United States Department of Justice

A Networking Tale ...

How I came to write this book is a story about networking. I was busy doing what I like to do best: supporting a professional colleague. Debra Snider and I met years ago when we were running legal departments for two Chicago-based companies. We probably had not seen one another in almost a decade. We had both left the practice of law, our paths no longer crossed, and we had fallen out of touch.

When I saw the announcement that Debra would be flying from Las Vegas to a meeting of the Chicago-based Senior Businesswomen's Forum to read from her new novel (she previously authored two professional books), I could not wait to attend the event to learn about her newest venture. As the evening unfolded, we hugged and reconnected, talking about mutual friends, colleagues, and acquaintances.

In the audience was Debra's friend Kathy Morris, legal career counselor and former head of the ABA's Career Resource Center. When I began chatting with Kathy she asked me: "Do you want to write a book for the ABA?" That hadn't crossed my mind. But my brain and my mouth evidentially had different ideas on the subject (not, I'm afraid, an uncommon phenomenon). As I was thinking, "No, I have no time or interest in doing that," I heard myself say, "Yes, I'd like to write a book on networking for lawyers." I was immediately told to speak to another audience member, Jill Eckert McCall of the ABA. Within five minutes, this book was born.

The moral of the story: when you support others—without looking for something in return—unexpected opportunities become available to you. This, as you will learn in the forthcoming pages, is at the heart of networking.

Chapter One:
Networking Defined

Justice Potter Stewart's best-known phrase resulted from his quandary over how to describe "hard-core" pornography. Unable to find a satisfactory definition, he simply declared: "I shall not today attempt further to define the kinds of materials I understand to be embraced ... But I know it when I see it."[1]

His sentiments are analogous to how lawyers think and feel about networking. It makes many of them squeamish. Those who don't understand what it means often find the idea offensive.

If this is you, then you're in for a pleasant surprise.

Glad-handing, pandering, and pushiness are neither networking skills nor prerequisites to successful networking (and are, in fact, really incompatible with it). Networkers are people who generate positive energy and demonstrate a genuine interest in talking to others. After an encounter with a good networker ends, you're left feeling that you've met someone you'd like to get to know better.

That person can and should be you.

What Is Networking?

Gary Pines likes to define networking (more precisely, the objective of networking as distinguished from its process) as follows:

"Building relationships to provide value to others."

---

[1] *Jacobellis v. Ohio*, 378 U.S. 184, 197 (1964) (Potter, J., concurring).

What pops out at you immediately when you see this definition?

- Is it the concept of building relationships?
- Or, is it the perhaps surprising clause "to provide value to others?"

Networking, if it is to be successful, involves thinking about others and how you can help them. That may be a shock to you. Most people misperceive networking as a process of immediately helping oneself through a few well-placed introductions at cocktail parties, conferences, or via a friend.

Implied, but not stated, in the "building relationships" part of the definition is the time commitment necessary for effective networking. Relationships are not built in five-minute increments with handfuls of people you meet for the first time in the midst of a large gathering. Networking does not work like speed-dating. Think of it more as like growing a healthy plant, which requires premium soil, lots of sunlight, a bit of plant food, and a few seasons to be nurtured. And like a charming garden in which each plant requires a slightly different assortment of nutrients and care, networking is a highly personalized style of interacting with others—learning what "nutrients" they need and what "flowers" appeal to you.

Dean John Garvey observes:

> "The term network or networking can be a gross way of describing interactions with others. What we're really talking about is relationships. Perhaps not as close as one's family or one's closest friends, but even a business relationship is a type of friendship. People who are good at making friends understand how to treat people. The bigger picture is to treat the people in your network the way you treat your friends. Be involved in their lives."

Jill Wine-Banks adds a twist to the definition:

> "Networking is the natural consequence of friendship and doing a good job. Both naturally create the connections you need."

John Mitchell offers yet another variation on the theme:

> "Networking is building relationships through helping people. You can't help someone if you don't know what that person needs. You must ask others about themselves to learn what they need."

Simply stated, helping others is at the heart of networking.

What Networking Is *Not*

Perhaps even more important than honing an exact definition of networking is to understand what networking is *not*.

Jonathan Asperger likes to point out the distinction between networking and selling:

> "Networking is about identifying and meeting the needs of others to establish and enhance relationships as distinguished from selling which is about identifying and meeting the needs of others to generate income."

Networking is not a sale; it's a joint venture. It's not adversarial; it's collaborative. Unlike a sales-driven activity, the goal is NOT revenue, but helping others.

Why Network?

When you picked up this book, you had certain expectations of potential benefits you might receive as a result of learning more about the art of networking. What were your networking goals?

_____

_____

_____

Over years of conducting networking training sessions, I have asked the participants to articulate their understanding of why people network—and what benefits they expect to receive from networking. Here are some of their answers:

- Increase options
- Meet people for resources
- Make connections
- Raise profile
- Make friends
- Support friends
- Create allies
- Diversify perspective
- Expand acquaintances
- Find mentors
- Learn about job opportunities
- Develop sources of information

Consider these additional reasons to network:

- Develop a network
- Create opportunities at your current job
- Gain higher professional visibility

- Solidify relationships with existing clients
- Enhance collegial relations
- Expand non-professional horizons
- Maximize career satisfaction
- Create possibilities otherwise not anticipated

Have your networking goals expanded having read these lists? If so, how?

_____

_____

_____

Networkers Around You

You also can think about networking in terms of that which good networkers do. John Mitchell provides this insight:

"A good way to understand networkers is to think about people who always have a good book or a new, trendy restaurant to recommend. They tell you about these books and dining spots because they think you will enjoy them—not to get something in return from you. That is what a networker does: gives for the joy of it without expecting something in return."

A common trait of a good networker is a good listener. Our ability to help another person is strongly tied to our ability to understand who they are and what they need.

Before moving to the next chapter, identify five people that you know (not necessarily friends), that you consider to be good networkers. Then identify the key traits or skills they use to assist them in being successful networkers.

Good Networkers That I Know	Traits/Skills
1.	
2.	
3.	
4.	
5.	

Do you share any common traits or skills with these people? If so, which ones?

_____

_____

_____

Are there skills that you want to develop to assist your networking endeavor? If so, which ones?

_____

_____

_____

Chapter Two:
The Study of Networking

If you still think of networking as undistinguished, as some lowbrow but necessary adjunct to becoming a more successful lawyer, then you may be surprised to learn that it's a subject of serious academic inquiry.

The academic study of networking began in the 1920s as an outgrowth of psychology and continues today in such diverse fields as business, anthropology, sociology, epidemiology and physics. According to one of the leading authorities on network theory, Professor Brian Uzzi:[2]

"In the 1920s one of Freud's students, interested in the fringes of society, mapped out relationships with people. He coined the concept of the sociogram, but his work was overshadowed by the excitement over Freudian psychology. At the same time, anthropologists were studying family connections and lineages."

Professor Uzzi explains that it was not until the 1960s that the academic community began the serious study of networking:

"Networking, as an academic discipline, was not really advanced until the studies of Stanley Milgram, a psychologist at Harvard University in the 1960s. Through sending packages to random people and asking them to forward the package, by hand, to someone specific, Milgram developed the concept of 'six degrees of separation'[3]

---

[2] Articles by Professor Uzzi include: "How to Build Your Network" with co-author Shannon Dunlap, December, 2005 *Harvard Business Review* and "The Interdisciplinary 'New' Science of Social Networks" with co-author Luis Amaral to be published in *Management's Science's* Special Issue on Complex Systems Across Disciplines in 2007.

[3] See: "Six Degrees of Lois Weisberg," January 11, 1999, *New Yorker*, Annals of Society, by Malcolm Gladwell. See also *The Tipping Point* by Malcolm Gladwell, Back Bay Books/Little, Brown and Company Time Warner Book Group, 2000, 2002.

based on this 'small world experiment.' The real social science of networking did not develop until later in the 1960s when physicist and sociologist Harrison White began studying statistical mechanics and conceptualized the social structures of networks. In the 1990s a group of physicists got interested in networks because of the Worldwide Web. They began to see connections between servers and web pages. Around the same time epidemiologists were studying social networks to understand the spread of AIDS."

Professor Jack Heinz is an authority on the application of social sciences to the study of law. Professor Heinz studies professional networks and has looked closely at criminal justice system[4] and lobbyist networks[5]. Professor Heinz observes:

"Professional networks are real. They have impact on matters of practical, business and political importance. One study demonstrated that networking relations spread information about the use of the 'poison pill' in corporate America. Those lawyers who were better networked were in a position to help their clients fend off takeovers and were more effective lawyers."

Professor Heinz further articulates the power of networks:

"Networks are communication structures and communication is closely related to power. Information is a resource and an asset. For a lobbyist to be effective, he or she must know what's going on. Connections control the information flow. You can't function in any complex system without knowing what's going on and you learn what's going on through networking."

---

[4] See: "Networks among Elites in a Local Criminal Justice System," by John P. Heinz and Peter M. Manikas, *Law and Society Review*, Volume 26, Number 4, The Law and Society Association.

[5] See: "Inner Circles or Hollow Cores? Elite Networks in National Policy Systems," by John P. Heinz, Edward O. Laumann, Robert H. Salisbury, Robert Nelson, *Journal of Politics*, Vol. 52, No. 2, May 1990, University of Texas Press.

The business community has more readily embraced the notion of utilizing networking than the professional community. But even in the business community, only recently has it been treated as a discipline. According to Professor Uzzi:

"The idea of networks has always been known to business people. But until the last ten years, their exposure had been hit or miss. There was no formal attention paid to the process. People were either born with the natural ability to connect with people or were lucky in their connections. Starting about ten years ago, several scientific principles and theories helped create this as a real discipline."

It is not necessary to understand networking theory to be a good networker, but all good networkers, either through instinct or training, apply the concepts underlying the theory: they connect people to others, move in more than one community or social circle, and develop meaningful relationships that provide mutual benefit.

Chapter Three:
Your Current Network

Most people are unaware of their potentially broad existing network. They are far too busy trying to figure out how to network with new people who are going to "change their lives." In order to network effectively, one must be aware of all of his or her *current* relationships.

You're thinking: "Wait, hold on, I need *new* people since I haven't been getting any networking value out of my current contacts. If I was getting networking value out of my current relationships, I wouldn't need to read a book on networking." Wrong. Networking is a mechanism for building relationships that add value to one another.

Friends and Friendship

Most people select their friends because of shared experiences and interests. Think about your true friendships and select one long-time, trusted friend.

Consider:

- A friend from grammar school
- An old neighborhood chum
- A sports teammate
- A high school cohort who was part of your crowd
- A college friend from your dorm freshman year
- A law school classmate who was a member of your study group
- Someone you met through your siblings or children
- Your next-door neighbor

Why did you choose that person to be your friend?

How did the friendship grow?

How willing are you to help your friend if you were asked?

How would you feel if your friend didn't ask you for help that you could have provided?

How willing do you think your friend would be to help you if you asked for help?

How would your friend respond if you didn't ask for help that your friend could have provided?

Now, how would you feel if your friend exploited your relationship for his or her personal advantage? Would you still consider this person a friend?

Implicit in our characterizations is that the **friendship has no ulterior motive**. The friendship itself is the end—it's not a means to the people our friend will introduce us to, the presents our friend will shower upon us, or how our friend will make us professionally successful.

What differentiates our true friends from the rest of the unknowns in our lives is the genuine feeling we carry with us that they would never abuse the relationship.

Mutual respect goes a long way in unlocking opportunities and uncovering potential sources of assistance, including our next job or our next piece of business.

So, let us become comfortable and commit to the notions that we should:

- Consider our friends as part of our network
- Not abuse relationships we have with any member of our network
- Try to provide value to all members of our network

Although very few members of our network will be or become our intimate friends, if we try to treat all members of our network with the kind of respect and mutuality we give our most intimate friends, we will develop and maintain very effective networks.

Beyond respect, list five characteristics of your friends or friendships that are critical to you. Be candid!

1. _____

2. _____

3. _____

4. _____

5. _____

Did your list include words such as:

loyal	honest	sincere	sympathetic
empathetic	helpful	fun	intuitive
trustworthy	dependable	caring	supportive
reliable	companionable	kind	unselfish

Keep this list handy to remind yourself of the traits and characteristics you should try to emulate as you network.

12 Magic Circles

One way to capture your current network is through a visual map. Consider mapping out your relationships in circles. Typically, I find that 12 circles are sufficient to gather one's preliminary resources. While I like to think of the circles as magic, the categories of the circles will vary from lawyer to lawyer because every person's network is, by definition, personal to that individual.

Additionally, the categories will evolve during one's lifetime. Michael Nemeroff comments:

> "Networking changes depending on the stage of your career. In the early stage, you should meet as many people as you can. In your mid-20s you should join auxiliary boards and enjoy the fun of planning parties and meeting interesting people. You should do well and do good at the same time. As your career develops, you should spend business time with people you can help and that can help you to develop mutually beneficial relationships."

Other changes may come from a more personal situation. For example, once a person is married, a spouse's friends or co-workers can become valuable categories in your network. Similarly, once you have children in playgroups or schools, you may add the parents of your children's friends as one of your circles.

Below you will find three example sets of circles representing a 20, 40 and 60-something lawyer. The changes in the categories are bolded for your reference.

Here is an example of a group of 12 magic circles for a lawyer in his or her late 20s:

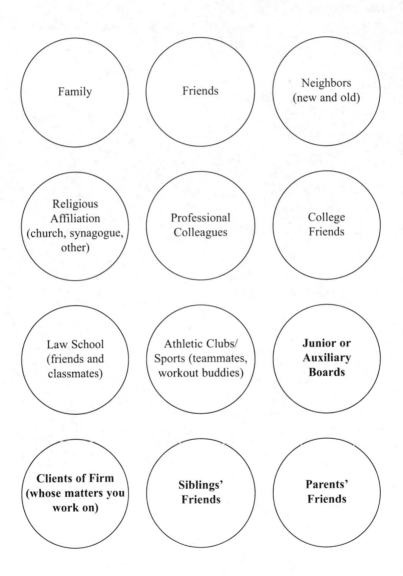

Here is an example of a group of 12 magic circles for a lawyer in his or her mid-40s:

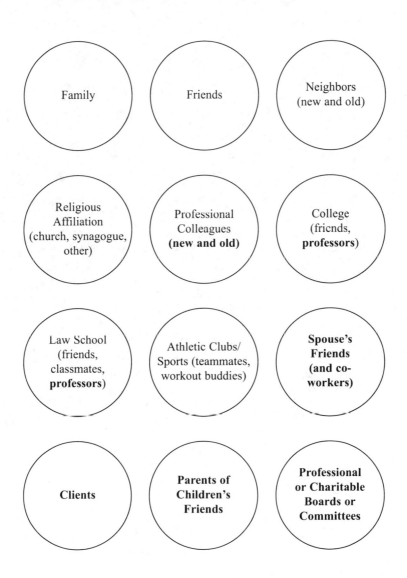

Here is an example of a group of 12 magic circles for a lawyer in his or her early 60s:

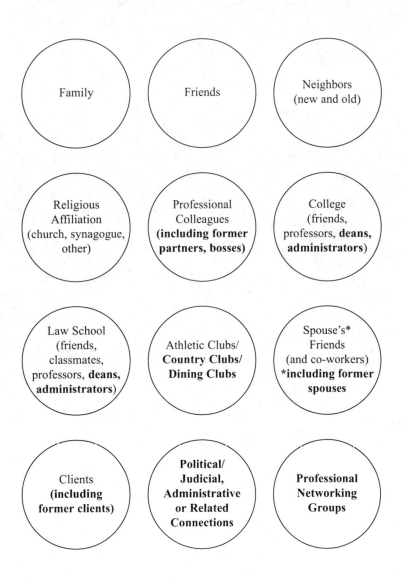

Family

Friends

Neighbors
(new and old)

Religious
Affiliation
(church, synagogue,
other)

Professional
Colleagues
**(including former
partners, bosses)**

College
(friends,
professors, **deans,
administrators**)

Law School
(friends,
classmates,
professors, **deans,
administrators**)

Athletic Clubs/
**Country Clubs/
Dining Clubs**

Spouse's*
Friends
(and co-workers)
***including former
spouses**

Clients
**(including
former clients)**

**Political/
Judicial,
Administrative
or Related
Connections**

**Professional
Networking
Groups**

Draw your 12 magic circles:

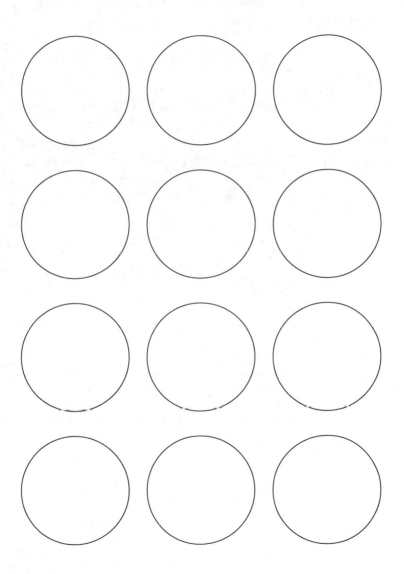

For each circle identified, list the names of ten people who fit within that category. *Do this reflexively without making judgments as to whom to include or exclude.* In other words, do not hesitate to include those:

- Who may not be valuable to you at this moment
- Whom you currently think you never want to connect with again
- Who you may be embarrassed to call or write after all these years

Just sit down and complete each category as the names enter your mind. Sometimes it helps if you think about your activities while active within that group. For example:

Law School
1. Study group member
2. Moot court partner
3. Roommate
4. Locker mate
5. Professor who mentored me
6. Guy from college who went to law school with me
7. Girlfriend who I reconnected with (and then lost touch with) at the last reunion
8. Member of pick-up basketball game on Friday nights
9. Classmate who sat next to me during torts
10. Friend I studied with for the bar exam

Twelve circles multiplied by ten names within each: that's your IMMEDIATE network of 120 people. Pretty amazing isn't it? Congratulate yourself on completing an exercise that most lawyers dread. Then date your worksheet so it will serve as a baseline reference for you.

Now, what should you do with your existing network? That, as you may have guessed, depends on where you are in your career and what your motivation was for networking in the first instance. For now, let's just assume that you wanted to get in on the networking bandwagon and you have no specific need (e.g., a job search) that motivated you to start networking. Here are some rules for using the network you just created.

Ten Rules of Networking

1. While this is your existing network as of today, not everyone will stay in your 12 circles even six months from now. Entire categories may disappear and new ones appear because your needs and capabilities will change. Note that during a job search, an extremely large network is critical. For business development, however, a very deep set of smaller relationships is preferable.

2. Even though some of these people are transitory, many will be permanent members of your network.

3. You will meet new people daily. Only time will tell who will become part of your network.

4. You will meet people who you want to be part of your network, but they won't become members because there is a lack of mutuality on their part. That's okay. Everyone can't fit everywhere. And you'll meet people who want you to be part of their network, and it won't happen for the same reason.

5. As you and your network friends grow and change, you will ask and give differently.

6. The intimacy of your connection and the caliber of your relationship will dictate your approach to members of your network.

7. You will never tap all the members of your network. Nor do you need to stay in contact regularly with all of them.

8. The list of 120 names you just developed is really only a small fraction of your existing network. You could probably create another category right now and fill it with another ten names.

9. Be mindful of how you interact with people in your network. Remember the pledge not to abuse any members of your network.

10. Always stay open to entering into others' networks.

Reconnecting with Your Existing Network

Before you begin reconnecting with your existing network, take some time to consider with whom you wish to reconnect and why. As a small step in this direction, select three people in your circles with whom you have been "out of touch," but with whom it would be fun to reconnect. Why would you enjoy re-establishing a connection? How would you go about establishing a connection—e-mail, phone call, letter, holiday card, surprise visit? When are you going to do this—today? Tomorrow? Next week?

Person	Reason	Contact Approach	Timing

Ironically, many people find it easier to just "write-off" people in their existing networks and start fresh with new people they meet. This is, in part, because none of us are able to stay in close contact with all of the people that waltz in and out of our lives. Rather than trying to do the impossible—stay closely connected or reconnect meaningfully with everyone in our existing network—try a compromise: superficial connection to some, non-connection with others (at least for now), and serious connection with a selected group. Here are a few examples of what to do with your law school classmates:

1. The annual holiday or New Year's card, whether a personal card, a business card, or a family letter.

✓ DO: send these to everyone in your network you truly want to connect or reconnect with at this time.

✓ DO: write a small personal note. Sign it even if your name is embossed on the card. Your comments can run the gamut from generic "happy holidays" to an invitation for a specific event. Here are some examples of what you can write to even long-lost law school classmates.

- I was thinking of you last week when I read that our [former classmate] is making a run for judge. Hope all's well with you. Give me a call if you have time for lunch one of these days.

- I miss late-night chats about [professor]'s antics. Are you free for coffee next week? I'd love to reconnect.

- I'll be flying into New York for a deposition on February 2nd. Any chance I can take you to dinner on the 1st?

- I hope you and your family are well. Wishing you a joyous holiday season and a New Year filled with peace, happiness, health and prosperity.

- I just moved to [firm]. Would you believe that [former classmate] came to the firm at the same time? We were just talking about you—how about drinks next week after the holidays?

- I was thinking about you the other day and can't believe we've lost touch—give me a call if you find a free moment and tell me what you've been up to these days.

- Our firm is hosting a seminar February 12th on "Selecting the Situs of a Trust." I'll be moderating and would love to have you as my guest. I'll give you a call/send you an e-mail next week to see if you're available. (*NOTE:* This example works particularly well if you're with a firm and your connection is an in-house counsel.)

✓ DON'T: mail a card that you haven't personalized. That is a waste of paper and postage.

✓ DON'T: send to someone who will not think of you as either a friend or active acquaintance. Do NOT blanket your entire law school class with these cards. Your recipients should be able to have a quick image of you in their mind the minute they see your name—and not need to scratch their heads trying to remember who you were!

✓ DON'T: pretend an intimacy that never existed, as that would seem artificial.

✓ DON'T: forget to send them a card again next year even if you failed to connect by phone or in person after sending the first card. Sometimes it takes years of superficially staying in touch before people find the need or desire to actually reconnect. An annual hello is still far better than a hello after a ten-year silence, especially if you will be requesting assistance from someone.

2. An e-mail, phone call, letter any time of the year.

✓ DO: compose carefully—even your opening lines for a phone call. This is especially true for someone with whom you have been out of touch with for a long time and with whom you had a good, but not intimate, relationship.

✓ DO: think of a "hook" for reconnecting—the more genuine the reason, the better the chance of truly re-establishing a relationship. In addition to the examples in the holiday letter list above, consider the following:

• You have read an article that is relevant to their firm, business or charity. Attach the article with some type of notation (e.g., good news, great victory, or congratulations).

- You have information about an opportunity that may be of value to them, such as a job lead for which they are particularly well-qualified.
- You want to introduce them to someone you think they can help (e.g., a college student who is writing a research paper on their area of expertise). *Caution:* it is more than permissible to ask people to help others, but be considerate to limit their time commitment and obligation. Say something like: "My wife's nephew is writing his college thesis on environmental issues and he wanted to ask you some questions that will take no more than ten minutes of your time."

3. An upcoming reunion. Most classes host them every five years.

   ✓ DO: attend.
   ✓ DO: send out a note asking if your friends plan on attending. Ask who else they know is going. Remember, the more people you know ahead of time who will be attending the event, the more comfortable you will be upon arrival.
   ✓ DO: suggest that you get together for drinks the night before. If that sounds like a good idea to your closest friend, offer to send the e-mail inviting all the rest.
   ✓ DO: ask if they're staying at a hotel. If so, you may want to coordinate hotels or even offer to share a room.
   ✓ DO: find out whether seats will be assigned. If so, work with the event coordinator to ensure that you are seated with friends.
   ✓ DON'T: carry law school emotional baggage with you.
   ✓ DON'T: drink too much or share intimacy that you will regret when the reunion is long over.

✓ DON'T: bad-mouth classmates. Not only is this bad form, it's dangerous; you never know who will appear in your life as your next partner or boss or colleague. Nor do you know who will repeat your comment to someone who would think less of you for insulting people.

✓ DON'T: pretend to know something or someone that you do not. You will lose credibility when the truth is revealed. Lawyers commingle and communicate regularly and it's a far smaller community than you might imagine.

✓ DON'T: forget to follow-up on any promises you made during the reunion. Failure to follow up will show your lack of follow-through and will often prove fatal to re-establish a meaningful relationship. Remember, networking is about providing benefit to others. Following up with a promise is the corner-stone of providing that benefit.

Reconnected: Now What?

First, recognize that you've joined the ranks of professional networkers—and mind you, this is only the third chapter!

Second, create and maintain a database (electronic or manual) of your network (see Chapter Ten).

Third, understand that you are now ready to move to developing networks with new people and forging new relationships.

How New and Deep Friendships and Business Relations Grow out of Networking

Expect complex and overlapping relationships to emerge with the people in your network. Here are testimonials from successful networkers:

Faye Knowles talks about developing, maintaining, and enjoying professional networks:

> "As a young lawyer, I joined a group of eight bankruptcy lawyers from different firms in the city. We'd eat dinner together about once a month. We really just came together as resources for one another: a safe place to ask questions so we wouldn't look dumb in front of our peers or partners at our own firms. Now, twenty years later, we still get together, but as a social group and as a business referral source. Whenever any of us is conflicted out of a matter, we first turn to one another to pass on the client opportunity."

David Brown finds that networking, business development, and friendship all meld together:

> "Most of my friends are my clients. Most of my clients have become my friends. I have limited time and energy. When I work this way, I'm always enjoying the people that I socialize with and with whom I work. But this requires a true commonality of interests, both personal and professional. For me, it's tying together coaching for my kids' teams, leading community efforts, supporting my friends and clients' causes. I have a real passion to help others. If we're all successful, we can all give more to philanthropy."

Michael Nemeroff describes his experience of the overlap of networking, business development, and friendship:

> "Most of my business contacts have become my friends. So I have the best of all worlds—a big part of my job is being with my friends."

Francesca Maher describes how work and friendship overlapped for her:

> "My 'gal pals' network was created by a series of friends and their friends—six degrees of separation. The commonality was our positive outlook and our desire for it to be a fun experience when we got together. We were smart, committed to both our families and our careers and wanted to be with other well-rounded successful women with a good sense of humor."

Carolyn Clift sums up the relationship between networking and friendship:

> "The fundamental theme around networking is friendship. You have to develop friendships for this to work. They do not need to be intimate, they can be professional only, but they need to be real friendships. They can't be mechanical. Otherwise you're using people. The key is authenticity."

Lee Miller talks about the growth of both personal and professional friendships:

> "My personality is to develop personal relationships. I never focused on 'the top of the house.' The best way to have close relationships is to grow with people. I always enjoyed the career moves my clients made. I followed them as they moved from company to company and would help them when they were between positions. I did not think of it as networking. I thought it was interesting and fun. And all those people are very loyal, both as clients and friends."

Keep these views in mind as you progress through this workbook. They will help you cultivate a more rewarding network.

Keeping Your Priorities Straight

Unless you are a full-time networker (and I have yet to meet someone who fits that description), it is not possible to develop and maintain deep relationships with all the people you know and meet. As with every other aspect of life, set your priorities and stick to them. While every moment of your life is an opportunity to meet or engage with someone, that does not mean that doing so is the best use of your time at that moment. If you have a brief filing deadline at 4 p.m. and you head out to a coffee shop at 1 p.m. for a mental break and a cup of coffee, that is not the time to start a networking conversation. If you promised to get home in time for your daughter's soccer game, accepting drinks with some buddies at the office as you're walking out the door is not the right time to become closer friends with your internal office network. And, if you're at a conference and can meet hundreds of people, be realistic: how many will you have the time, inclination, and energy to maintain in your network?

Chapter Four:
Barriers and Opportunities

Karma, the Favor Bank and the Golden Rule

Most effective and well-liked networkers are atypically generous. They give without expectation of reciprocity. Ray Bayley articulates the concept:

> "Don't ever look for the quid pro quo; make an effort to help anyone who asks for help. By the same token, don't ever be afraid to ask for help not knowing how you will be able to help the person back."

Similarly, Dean John Garvey notes:

> "Your first thought should be what could you do to help someone because you care about him or her. It's trickier and there's a bit more tension when there's a business relationship involved, but even then, it's very important not to get hung up on keeping score."

Carolyn Clift sees this as a part of something bigger:

> "I believe in the higher order of things. When I meet someone and they come into my life a second time, I wonder why and how we are connected. Invariably something good comes out of it. The more attuned you are to people you meet, the more able you are to see the threads of connection, even if it's just for a short time. Quid pro quo expectations are political and not networking. In networking, giving without getting back is ok."

Jerold Solovy has enjoyed more than 50 years as a highly respected trial attorney. A dean among networkers, he has a simple and long-standing philosophy about doing favors for others:

> "My father never passed up a chance to do a favor. The world is a system of favors. There are good favors (kindnesses) and bad favors (bribes). My dad taught us about the importance of doing the good favors."

FOOD FOR THOUGHT: The best networkers rarely ask for assistance. They don't need to. Yet they get leads, referrals, and job offers all the time. Why do you think that is?

_____

_____

_____

The answer may surprise you. Generosity creates its own reward. Some people describe it as Karma, others as paying into the favor bank, and still others see it simply as an expression of the Golden Rule, "doing for others what you would have them do for you." Generous people are well-liked, well appreciated, and long remembered.

In Chapter Three we spoke about friendships, mutuality and respect. It is completely appropriate to ask for assistance (e.g., for a referral or a job lead) as long as we are not abusive or manipulative in our requests. Relationships, whether business or personal, consist of giving and getting. It is unnecessary, and probably unrealistic, to expect to give and get at the same exact time.

FEAR and FUN of Networking

Gary Pines suggests the acronym **FEAR** to explain why people do not engage in networking:

Failure
Embarrassment
Anxiety
Rejection

When taken as a whole, they can serve as powerful deterrents to initiating any networking effort. Take a moment for serious reflection. Do you experience any of these emotions when you consider undertaking any networking efforts? List them in order of interference with your activities.

1. _____

2. _____

3. _____

4. _____

Most of you will have selected at least one potential emotional roadblock. If you are in the lucky group of people who never experience these fears, skip this paragraph. For the rest of you, listen up:

- Networking is not a job interview
- Networking is not a performance evaluation
- Networking is not an athletic competition
- Networking is not a sales pitch
- Networking is not an entry exam to an exclusive private school or club
- Networking is NOT COMPETITIVE

The only person who knows if you're a winner is you. Networking, honestly, is a safe activity. Here is my promise to you: with the right attitude, a good elevator pitch (described in Chapter Five), a prepared conversational approach, and a consistent follow-up, you will NOT experience failure, embarrassment, anxiety, or rejection.

What to Do About External Barriers to Networking

At times you may encounter externally imposed barriers. It is often one's attitude towards those limitations that is critical to successful networking. Some of the women and minorities quoted in this book shared valuable insights on this sensitive subject. Their advice is compelling to everyone.

Manuel "Manny" Sanchez observes:

> "I never felt that my ability to network was adversely affected by my ethnicity or gender or age. To the contrary, I read the articles in the mid-80s that projected the rapid growth of the Hispanic population and a light bulb went off in my head. I knew then as I know now that there was a dearth of Hispanic business leaders and I viewed this not as a liability but as an opportunity to exploit. Luckily the baby boomer generation has been more willing to embrace diversity not as affirmative action, but how it impacts the bottom line. The United States population of clients, customers and workforce is steadily growing for minorities: African Americans, Asians and Hispanics."

Stephanie Scharf explains her views on networking for women:

> "I felt strongly about advancing the role of women in the

legal profession. A decade ago a lot of women lawyers in firms and corporations were hired at every level, but for multiple reasons they did not stay in high-powered positions. The National Association of Women Lawyers (NAWL) offers women a safe place to come together to advance their careers. I know that NAWL has opened up women's minds to opportunities they didn't realize they had and provided skills and information to help them succeed. The network NAWL provides is both professionally and personally satisfying."

Notwithstanding Ms. Scharf's deep commitment to the specialty bar, she is equally convinced of the importance of the American Bar Association for all lawyers:

"I am an active member of both the National Association of Women Lawyers and the American Bar Association. I strongly believe in general bar groups while also seeing the place for specialty bar groups."

Cornell Boggs provided a practical suggestion to help minorities determine if their perceived barriers or limitations are real or self-imposed:

"Minorities sometimes do not know if their opportunities arc actually limited because of their ethnicity. It is important for them to ask other minorities, or other trusted colleagues or resources, such as the Minority Corporate Counsel Association or the Charting Your Own Course Foundation to see if they are experiencing a problem that any lawyer in their circumstance would experience or whether they are truly experiencing a block or limitation because of their ethnicity. And, if they are truly limited as a result of ethnicity, they need to move to another organization to move forward in their career."

Dean Joe Knight talks about networking challenges faced by women and attorneys of color:

> "For women attorneys and attorneys of color who are often not part of mainstream business fraternities, it takes a little longer to become successful at business development through networking. Every professional needs to go through the growing pains of learning how to meet people and to 'schmooze' with them. If you cannot 'schmooze,' you cannot develop business. Frequently students do not understand that being brilliant is not enough to succeed in the business of legal practice. You must be personable, charming and communicative, and hard-working."

Dean Knight acknowledges the difficulty students experience as a result of their difference from the majority, but nonetheless advises that this is not a barrier to accept:

> "It is always easier to be with people who have similar backgrounds and interests. Students of color often put themselves in those groups. So do most people, whether Jewish or Christian, gay or straight, liberal or conservative. It is important to learn to become a 'risk-taker' going beyond the familiar and learning to make contacts with people outside of your comfort group."

Veta Richardson observes that minorities must learn to overcome the self-imposed impediment of feeling different:

> "There are probably a good number of minorities who feel intimidated or apprehensive by being in crowds of all majority. They need to overcome this feeling by practice. This is necessary or you will find yourself excluded. Even thought I have all the skills, I can still feel uncomfortable in an old-line private club that feels exclusive. Or worse, where the only minorities besides me are there solely in service."

While Ms. Richardson believes that women and minorities need to participate in majority networking settings, she does not believe that this participation should be at the expense of the individual's own values and sensibilities:

> "No one can be influential playing a game made out of someone else's rules. If women or minorities want to have power we won't be effective and diversity will not be reflected if you're trying to fit into a box not designed for us. I'm optimistic that if I remain true to myself and what interests me, it will make me more interesting to others. My goal is to be in a position of influence and that means I do things I enjoy—like getting a manicure rather than playing golf. I don't want to cede over who I am to make a relationship. If networking is about expanding your circle of influence, you cannot move forward if you're not true to yourself."

Professor Nancy Rapoport notes that while Dean:

> "I encouraged our law students to join student groups that made them feel 'safe' or 'at home.' At Houston, we have specialty groups of Hispanics, Asians, gays and lesbians, African Americans, and many others. These groups make the individuals feel welcome because of their shared experiences and their vested interest in seeing one another succeed. They allow students to talk in shorthand and let their guard down. Yet, it is equally important for students to network across groups as opportunities often come from people very different from themselves."

Is there a lesson to be learned about status barriers? One's status can be a true initial barrier. For those with a status barrier, successful networking may require the individual to go a greater distance to reach that point outside his or her comfort zone to find the commonality that eliminates the impact of the barrier.

Networking Should Be Enjoyable

Rather than being a dreaded chore, networking should be seen as a pleasant opportunity. Those people who are most likely to succeed at networking efforts are, not surprisingly, those who find it fun. Many people have asked me: Is it possible to enjoy networking?

Enjoying networking does not require a vivacious personality. Nor does it require exceptional looks, brains, wardrobes or wealth. What it does require is summarized in a second acronym, **FUN**:

> **F**ocused attention, especially LISTENING
> **U**nderstanding the opportunities to help others
> **N**eed to enjoy meeting **N**ew people

Every lawyer is trained to focus. It's essential to the practice. The only difference between focus in the context of the practice and focus in the context of networking is that the subject is a person rather than a document, a transaction, or a case.

Every lawyer is trained to understand. It's the result of focus. And as with focus, the difference with networking is understanding someone's needs rather than the nuances of a transaction or case.

And finally, every successful lawyer is trained to tackle new experiences. No two transactions or cases are ever the same; lawyers are always learning. It's no different with networking—except that the subject is a person.

In other words, networking engages the very skills at which lawyers excel. And if you think about it, those skills make the practice of law fun. It's no different with networking.

Once you understand that, it becomes obvious that successful networking doesn't require you to be anything other than who you are. You can be shy, bookish, and introverted and still be a terrific networker. Networking is based on *your* group of contacts and on *your* activities, whether daily, occasional, annual, or one-time. The networking exchanges are focused with people *you* encounter.

Jonathan Asperger believes lawyers are uniquely positioned for networking:

1. Lawyers are situated within a matrix of professionals and leading business people
2. They engage clients primarily though one-to-one professional relationships
3. Their work gives them an opportunity to see the big picture
4. Many of their clients view them as counselors
5. Top lawyers become trusted advisors

Many lawyers enjoy networking because it is a mechanism for building relationships. Some are temporary; some last a lifetime. They shift as your life and the lives of those around you change.

The Honorable Judge Joan Gottschall describes a fun aspect of networking:

"The networking process is fun because you have interactions with lots of people talking about you and your objectives. It is wonderful to feel connected with other people."

Similarly, from Francesca Maher:

"My gal pals network is one of the most personally rewarding. We help each other's charities, sometimes assist with each other's careers and sometimes we just have an enjoyable dinner together. My network makes my life more fun."

After engaging in the process, you too, may agree that networking is fun.

What Are Networking Types?

When you think about people with whom you would like to network, what kinds of people (or personality traits) would appeal to you?

- Are they similar or different to you in their career stages? Personality styles?
- What about their hobbies? Charities? Family life (e.g., single, young children, taking care of parent)?
- Does the uniqueness of people intrigue you—the more exotic the better? Or do you honestly prefer to be with people who are more like you than unlike you?

There is no universal right answer. Your answer should be the one that works for you. Maximize your ability to network by understanding the kinds of people that interest you and with whom you feel comfortable interacting. Most of the people with whom you interact daily—such as relatives, supervisors, peers, clients, adversaries, and competitors—were not chosen by you, yet you routinely and effectively engage and interact with them.

As you find yourself more comfortable with the process of interacting with people as a networker, you will begin to care far less about peoples' styles or types. But to begin this analysis, consider the types of people with whom you would feel most comfortable.

List the personality traits, attitudes or styles that most appeal to you (e.g., outgoing, humorous, religious, athletic):

_____

_____

_____

List the type of people that appeal to you (e.g., occupation, education level, physical description):

_____

_____

_____

Now, be fair to yourself. Be honest. List the types of people or personality traits that simply annoy you. Here's your own private list of the kinds of people with whom you do not want to network:

1. _____

2. _____

3. _____

4. _____

5. _____

To increase the likelihood of having **FUN** when you network, seek out the kinds of people that appeal to you.

Where to Network

Networking, at its most basic level, starts as nothing more than a conversation between people. And, since a conversation can take place almost anywhere, every venue provides a networking opportunity. Many people erroneously think that great networkers are people who can work a room without breaking into a sweat and collect dozens of business cards. While there are some networkers who can successfully practice this style of networking, they are in the minority.

Remember, as we earlier discussed, the only way that networking can work for you is if you're being yourself. This means that networking may take place with a group of guys watching a football game, with a few women getting their nails done, with couples dining in someone's home, or with former colleagues enjoying lunch. Some lawyers truly love networking at a large conference, wedding, or cocktail party. And for others, networking works best at their gym, the local coffee shop, or the train station.

Even sitting in a first class cabin flying across the ocean can provide opportunity. Networking locations don't have to be circumstantial; they can be selected. Nina Stillman remembers:

> "As a young lawyer, I always paid (out of my own salary) to upgrade to first class. I knew I'd have a more comfortable seat to work in and a captive audience with a likely top executive or general counsel."

Think about your daily activities. Are there places where you routinely find yourself engaging in easy small-talk with relative strangers? Think of networking as comfortable chit-chat. For example, do you find yourself asking a barista whether she saw any good movies over the weekend or talking to the person working out at the treadmill next to yours what he thinks about the gym's music selection or waving hello to the same neighbor every day as you head to your office?

List some of the situations where you feel at ease in your daily routine and find yourself chatting casually with others:

_____

_____

_____

Here are some additional situations to consider:

- Events outside of your daily routine
- The pool while on vacation
- Your child's soccer game
- Your parents' annual holiday party

List three additional situations:

1. _____

2. _____

3. _____

Your networking efforts in venues that put you at ease will be more effective than at events that make you cringe because you will be more relaxed. Seek out these places.

Typical venues and activities for lawyers provide networking opportunities. For example:

- Daily professional activities in the workplace
- Professional meetings and conferences
    - Bar association
    - Association of Corporate Counsel
- Professional or trade association boards

Don't forget about venues and activities outside the work context:

- Socializing with family, neighbors and friends
    - School parties
    - Holiday parties
    - Block parties
- Charity boards
- Sports clubs or events

Let's move now to techniques designed to make networking easier—and thereby more **FUN**.

Chapter Five
The Nuts and Bolts of Networking

How to Prepare for Networking Conversations

Before you begin a conversation, you must always carry in your mind these basic principles:

1. Networking is mutual and reciprocal

2. Give before getting

3. Half the trick to a good conversation is asking open-ended questions

4. The other half of the trick to a good conversation is listening well

5. The key to an engaged conversation is to find the point of commonality

REMEMBER: You were given two ears and only one mouth for a reason: listen twice as much as you talk!

LISTENING TIPS:

- Do not interrupt—lawyers frequently feel compelled to finish others' stories
- Respond to what others say without self-aggrandizing stories in which you are the hero

If you think about a successful conversation from the other person's viewpoint, it will probably include learning something useful or receiving assistance, whether a connection for a new job or a lead for a new client.

Gary Pines has another apt acronym: networking encounters are a means to **RAISE** one's profile:

Refer people to new contacts
Advise when requested
Invite people to functions; **I**nform people of opportunities
Support people emotionally, both in good and bad times
Extend **E**mployment assistance

Perhaps you find it surprising, but helping others is one of the best ways to raise one's own profile!

The Elevator Pitch

The anxiety-producing question you're invariably asked in social or professional contexts is:

"What do you do?"

It seems to invite either responses that provide too little data (e.g., "I'm a lawyer") or too much information (e.g., "I'm a lawyer, practicing at Little Known Firm, specializing in Lesser Known Area, and one of my new associates/old partners, …"). The only thing worse than being asked that question is *not* being asked it, because now you're going to have to communicate the same information unsolicited.

Many people have come to understand the need to develop an "elevator pitch"—a quick response to the "What do you do?" question. As noted earlier, an elevator pitch is an indispensable tool to eliminating **FEAR**.

The concept of the elevator pitch is simple: an interesting self-description suitable to an encounter in an elevator with a stranger with 15 floors in which the connection opportunity will be made or lost.

It only takes one floor to identify your profession and organization. That's not the problem. The problem is how to describe your profession and organization in a manner that distinguishes you from your counterparts at other firms or organizations, impresses a potential client, and forges a connection by the 15th floor. Sharan Ilene Tash says:

> "Networking for lawyers and beauty salon owners is all the same. The biggest mistake a person makes is saying, 'Hi. My name is Sally. I'm a lawyer.' The reason it's a mistake is that if the listener already has a lawyer, the speaker has done nothing to pique that person's interest. So, what an attorney needs to do is within the first 15 seconds of meeting someone, he or she needs a 'hook' to get the other person to listen. We get inundated with thousands of advertisements a day. What will stand out? That takes time to figure out. A lawyer, or anyone else, needs to connect with her passion and their work. You need to think of what you are most proud of and connect that with your business."

So let's consider a better way of introducing yourself than: "Hi. I'm a lawyer and I work at such and such firm..." Consider these variations and a second approach:

- "I work with developers and investors on maximizing their investments in commercial real estate deals. I've been in this industry for more than a decade and simply love my work." (Note the avoidance of the word transactions, which many people outside the legal field consider legalese. Also note that you need not identify your firm or even mention that you are a lawyer in some situations).

When identifying yourself as a lawyer seems indicated by the circumstance of the conversation, consider this version:

- "I work with developers and investors on maximizing their investments in commercial real estate deals. I've been in this industry for more than a decade and have been fortunate during that time to work at a mid-size firm that specializes in these kind of projects." (Only identify your firm by name if it is relevant to the conversation.)

Another approach:

- "I work with start-up companies and help protect them before they even open their doors. Luckily, I am fortunate to have a group of partners with different expertise and talents who work with me to help solve business problems in areas such as financing, leasing, and employment matters…"

The truth about elevator pitches, as so eloquently explained above by Ms. Tash, is that you need to describe the work you do in a way that shows *your* passion and *your* capability. There is no "standard" description—for it to be real and meaningful, it needs to describe you and your attitude about your work.

HINT #1: If you find "What do you do?" off-putting, so do others—remember not to ask that of someone else. If, for example, you are talking to another lawyer, whether inside or outside of your organization, perhaps you can phrase a "feeler" question along these lines:

- "What is it that you like about practicing law?"
- "How did you develop your area of expertise?"

HINT #2: The best way to perfect one's elevator pitch is through practice. Start by pitching to a family member or neighborhood pet (seriously), and then move to the mirror when you feel that your pitch can be delivered smoothly. Note and adjust your facial expressions. Finally, practice with your spouse, child, sibling, or close friend. Once you are comfortable in front of someone who knows you well, you're ready for prime time: giving your elevator pitch to a complete stranger.

How to Enjoy a Conversation at a Networking Event

Although the elevator pitch can be closely connected with the opening line of a conversation, they are not one and the same. The elevator pitch is typically a well-conceived and well-rehearsed description of what you do professionally, but is not necessarily delivered at the beginning of a conversation. It is part description, part hook, and part sales pitch. A smooth, well-rehearsed elevator pitch helps in two situations:

1. To respond to the ubiquitous "What do you do?" inquiry and
2. To use at networking events when everyone goes around the table/room and introduces himself or herself.

The general conversation, discussed directly below, is more interactive in nature and may not even include a person's elevator pitch.

For many lawyers, starting a conversation is the most troublesome part of the entire networking experience. If they could only find a good opening line, some believe, the rest would flow naturally. For others, particularly the more introverted lawyers who tend to shy away from meeting strangers, even an opening line is insufficient. They worry about how to approach a stranger, how to break into a group of people, how to keep the dialogue flowing, and—if they get past those barriers—how to exit from the encounter.

To avoid the anxiety and discomfort of entering into conversations with new people, lawyers often find themselves doing one of several things during a break in the sessions or between structured activities. Are you guilty of any of these behaviors?

- Going to the Internet kiosk
- Charging to the nearest window to check your handheld for e-mails
- Heading out to the hallway to make a call
- Searching for the first familiar face and making a beeline to that person
- Standing in line to wait for the dinner buffet to open
- Sitting in a corner, opening your briefcase and furiously working on a document
- Stretching your legs on a solo walk outside of the meeting place
- Ditching the event to go out to lunch with a good friend who works near the conference

If you recognize any of those behavior patterns in yourself, it's time to create new habits. Here's how:

1. Acknowledge that the only way to expand your network is to meet new people.

2. Remember what it's like to argue in court or negotiate a deal. When you are prepared, the stage fright disappears.

3. Prepare by researching the event *before* attending. While some conferences will not provide attendee

lists in advance, many others will if you place a two-minute phone call to the conference organizer. Even if you are unable to secure the list of attendees, you will have ready access to the list of topics and speakers. Here are some of the quickest ways to research the individuals or their companies:

- Perform a search engine inquiry
- Read the company's website, with specific attention to the organization's press release or news section and the company's philosophy
- Ask friends and colleagues if they know anything about the people or organizations
- Read the *Wall Street Journal, Financial Times, American Lawyer, Corporate Counsel Magazine, Inside Counsel,* and *Harvard Business Review* routinely (even if you are not reading about the person or company specifically, you will have a broad understanding of most industries and conference topics)

4. Decide not only which sessions you want to attend ahead of time, but more importantly which people you want to meet or visit.

As an example, let us assume you work for a law firm and you are attending a conference where an old classmate who is now in-house counsel of a potential client is speaking. What should you do?

GOOD: Look for your friend at the conference. Presumably he or she will be happy to see you and, at the very least, you two will reconnect sufficiently for a follow-up conversation after the conference.

BETTER: Call or send an e-mail in advance of the conference, letting the person know you will be attending, and set up a meeting time before you even arrive. Advance communication lets your contact know that you are interested in meeting with him or her (and avoids the risk that you will come off at the conference as opportunistically cornering them). It sends a message that you are strategic in the way you attend conferences and eliminates the anxiety over whether you will be able to carve out time with your client/friend. It also allows you more control over your time to meet new people, as you will not be spending all the breaks seeking out your "target."

BEST: Sort through the attendee list to find another person you know who will be attending the event. Send both the speaker and this other person e-mails suggesting that if they are not yet acquainted that you would like to introduce them at the conference.

5. Recognize that you will not be the only person at this event who is nervous or uncomfortable about approaching strangers. Look for someone who appears to be just as shy. Approach that person first. The trick is to ask questions that require more than a simple yes or no answer. Design your opening question to start a dialogue.

For example, an opening line to introduce yourself to that person clutching his or her glass of wine at the bar and nervously looking around the room is: "Hi. What do you think about the wine?"

Alternatively:

• What do you think is on those sandwiches?
• Where have you found connectivity at this hotel?
• Which local restaurants have you tried?

6. Even if you are not shy, prepare an opening line that will work for most of the people you meet. Remember: the goal for any networking encounter is to engage the other person in conversation. Here are some examples:

- Have you ever heard [the speaker] before? What did you think of [the speaker's] presentation?
- I'm not sure that I have the time to commit if I join this subcommittee. How useful do you find the organization's resources in your practice?
- This is the first time I attended this conference. Who are some of the speakers I should make sure to hear?
- What brings you to this meeting?

Here are two helpful and related hints:

HINT #1: Remember, the goal of every conversation is to find commonality. In this regard, women seem to be naturals. Put a group of professional women together and someone will invariably comment something like "stunning bracelet" or "beautiful scarf" without getting too personal (e.g., "Are you married?"). Men, and do forgive me for the stereotypes here, tend to converse most effectively when discussing things outside of themselves, such as sports (e.g., "So, what do think of the Cubs *this* year?"). Stereotypes aside (plenty of men like to talk about their families and personal matters and an equal number of women enjoy playing and discussing sports), the key, again, is to find common ground.

HINT #2: Pay attention. Most people give clear signs when they are connecting with you or the topic at hand. Seek out those clues. For example, notice when someone appears more animated or enthusiastic during a discussion, and be sensitive to your own energy level—if you seem bored, that will be clearly communicated.

Veta Richardson describes in detail how she overcame her discomfort of talking to strangers at large gatherings:

> "I was the first person in my family to go to college. I knew that my dad networked to expand his clients and business but I had no idea what people meant about networking in college. I knew I was supposed to meet people but I was not sure why. In the early stages of my college career I was dumbfounded. I did not know how to put forth the right social skills. So, when I went to law school I decided I needed to figure out this networking business. I lacked any confidence to walk up to a stranger so I forced myself to go to the Baltimore conference center to non-legal conventions where I knew no one. I decided that social skills are learned behavior and I could teach myself to feel more comfortable. I set goals such as introducing myself as a law student to three people. Then I gave myself permission to leave. After several conventions I realized that networking was really just people making small talk. So I figured I could ask basic questions such as, 'Where are you from?' Then, I developed two responses. If I was familiar with their hometown I would talk about the places and people I knew. If I didn't know about their hometown I asked them to describe it to me. In other words, I mapped out a reasonable small talk exchange. At some point, it just became natural for me to talk to people."

Even when people have attained a high degree of competence as professional speakers and industry leaders, they can still experience anxiety when meeting new people. With great candor, Dean Joe Knight describes his feelings:

> "I'm nervous every time with butterflies when I make a new speech or meet new people. But I know that I still must deliver the speech and meet the people. You must make connections when you walk into a room. You have to be comfortable with yourself to engage in a conversation. You need not be the luckiest or the smartest or the most talented person out there. But you must be willing to put yourself in the moment and to extend yourself to people."

7. The next tricky part comes shortly after you deliver your opening line and engage in the first few seconds of dialogue: introducing yourself. Introductions can be difficult for lawyers, particularly in non-legal networking events. You can use your elevator pitch right here if it feels right to do so. When you describe yourself as someone who works in an industry helping others, you leave an opening for the other person to inquire: "Oh? In what capacity?" And therein lies the opportunity to describe in more detail that you are an attorney, with a firm or at a corporation, and the kinds of clients with whom you work.

8. Ironically, some of the worst networkers at conferences are the people best positioned to take advantage of the networking opportunities: the speakers. They tend to huddle with the other speakers (who they know from the conference planning calls or the dinner preceding the event). And, that's if they even bother to stay at the event. Speakers are notorious for running in just before their sessions start and departing at the conclusion of their remarks.

9. Even "important" people need to remember to contin-
   uously build their networks. Perhaps you have seen
   rainmakers fall out of favor and struggle as they seek
   out new firms. Or maybe you've seen prestigious
   general counsel lose their jobs with the advent of a
   new CEO. Sticking around at conferences, especially
   when you are a presenter, is a critical way to make
   connections that you may need some day.

After the Opening Line: Now What?

While the opening lines are essential, the questions that follow are the keys to establish the networking relationship.
Asking focused questions helps unlock the networking potential in any exchange.

All too often, networking opportunities are missed because
people cannot determine how they can actually assist another
person. An essential mechanism for achieving this goal is by
asking simple, focused questions about their needs. Let's
practice.

Pretend you are networking with an accountant. What types
of questions might you ask?

_____

_____

_____

Here is one suggestion:

- "How would I know if I were talking to someone who would be an ideal customer for you?"

Assume you are talking to a salesman in the automotive industry. What types of questions might you ask?

_____

_____

_____

Here is one suggestion:

- "Who are your key suppliers?"

Maybe you are engaged in discussion with a vice-president of marketing in the food industry. What types of questions might you ask?

_____

_____

_____

Here is one suggestion:

- "How has your industry changed over the past five years?"

Caution About Cocktail Party Etiquette

Jill Wine-Banks offers important cautionary advice about networking at cocktail parties:

> "If you are clumsy at networking, you'll damage your cause. For example, it's really insulting and annoying at a cocktail party if you're talking to someone but always looking over his or her shoulder to see who you can talk to next."

Remember that you only need to make two or three good connections. You get no extra points for shaking hands with everyone at an event. The important goal is to make meaningful connections and determine the appropriate follow-up to ensure the connection will provide mutual benefit.

After the Conversation

A critical distinction between a simple conversation and networking is the follow-up required. If you do not follow up, you did not network. Many professional networkers use this rule of thumb: three touches within the first three months of meeting a new person. For a more detailed discussion, including an effective use of the other person's business card, please refer to Chapter Ten.

Chapter Six:
Internal Networking

Whether you are a newly minted lawyer, recently switched firms, moved from a firm to a company, or transitioned into a totally new career, this is an opportune time for you to begin a whole new chapter of networking.

Internal networking is a critically important, and often over-looked, aspect of networking. It is how careers are shaped and developed. It significantly influences one's enjoyment of the workplace. And, ironically, it is often the key to moving to a different and better job opportunity.

Gary Pines notes the importance of internal networking before embarking on an external networking effort:

> "You need to be internally networked before you are exter-nally networked or you may fall on your face. Internally you need three things: (1) have a vibrant contact list of col-leagues; (2) build relationships by asking questions and not by telling them how great you are and then doing favors for people ('give before you get'); and (3) have a consistent routine to periodically stay in touch."

John Mitchell notes the business development aspect of inter-nal networking:

> "Internal networking is the most important thing for any lawyer in a firm of 25 people or more. It is far more important than external networking. All marketing con-sultants will tell you that it's easier to get additional busi-ness from an existing client than it is to get business from a new client. Even recognizing that law firms cannot always service all of a client's work, most firms

do only a small percentage of the possible work they
could do for a client. The reason many firms fail to effectively cross-market is because the partners do not trust
each other. If attorneys spend time networking within
their firms, they can develop the strong relationships with
their partners that are a pre-requisite for cross-selling."

The Need to Network Inside Law Firms

Lee Miller identifies the importance of internally networking
at several levels:

"You should always network at three levels: your relationships with your counterparts, your relationships with
the top people and your relationships with the people
below your level. One of my role models taught me this
critical lesson: no one is beneath you."

David Brown believes deeply in the value of internal networking:

"Young lawyers need to understand that they have many
resources in their firms and they do not need to feel iso-
lated in their networking efforts. They should ask the
firm's partners for help in their networking efforts. I
deeply believe that partners need to provide opportunities
for the younger lawyers that service their clients."

Debbie Berman agrees:

"It is very important to bring value to all members of your
firm, not just your peers or the people above you. In a big
firm, a lawyer needs to interact beyond his or her practice
group. You need to know the lawyers and the support
staff in other areas. You need to be involved in firm
activities such as recruiting and associate development."

Michael Nemeroff also explains the importance of internal networking:

> "It is important to know the members and resources of your firm. This is how you can promote what others do in the firm and how they can promote you. It also allows rainmakers to better cross-sell to their own clients."

Another often-overlooked aspect of internal networking relates to mergers between law firms. Mergers can be particularly frustrating for a small firm that is acquired by a significantly larger firm. Concerted efforts by both firms can significantly increase the likelihood of achieving the merger goals.

Allan Katz was the managing partner of small law firm when it merged into a significantly larger law firm. He shares his wisdom in this arena:

> "The networking goal as the managing partner of the smaller firm that is being absorbed in a merger is to meet with all of the shareholders from the larger firm—at their offices to share your practices and how they relate to the larger firm's clients. We targeted a person from each office after our meetings to be our 'go to' person. This resulted in immediate goodwill and a heightened awareness of how our two firms would benefit from one another."

Never underestimate the importance of "playing nice" in your own working environment. People always are more willing to work with others who show a positive attitude and embrace the organization over the individual.

Specific Tips for In-House Lawyers

For in-house counsel, internal corporate networking, both within and outside the legal department, is critical for job security, promotion, and status.

Marla Persky explains her approach to internal networking:

> "Be as generous to the people below you as the people above you. The people above you will likely remain above you or move out of the organization. But the people below you may surpass you in the organization."

Ms. Persky also finds internal networking a pleasurable activity:

> "Personally, I get satisfaction out of seeing people that I've helped along the way succeed."

Echoing these sentiments is Francesca Maher. She notes:

> "I had a very rewarding experience creating a forum for senior women in my company. Our initial group was 21 women. Five or six years later when the group ended there were 120 women. I felt that I made a difference in the lives of the women in my organization."

Anna Richo articulates the career enhancing aspect of internal networking:

> "Most lawyers coming in-house are not cognizant of the importance of internal networking. And, even if they are consciously aware, most assume that the networking is simply within the legal function. That's a big mistake. From a career standpoint, the fastest way to advance is when business clients tell the general counsel that you are

an important part of their business team, contributing to the unit's growth."

Ms. Richo describes the scope of the internal networking process beyond the legal function:

"Business clients are not simply the sales and marketing teams. They include every function that is non-legal, such as manufacturing, R & D, finance and IT. Ideally, you will position yourself so that key business leaders are talking about you. To achieve this, you need to recognize opportunities to interface with these leaders. Some of the best opportunities come when working on a significant piece of litigation or managing a fast tracked deal. These are the circumstances when you can build a reputation and people can talk about your help during a difficult or critical time."

Networking in Law Schools

Law schools are natural internal networking incubators. To those readers who are current law students, heed the advice of some of the well-regarded deans quoted below.

Dean David Van Zandt explains:

"Arguably law school is all about professional networking. The real value you get out of a top law school is being put with people of promise and the opportunity to develop relationships with these people to be harvested in later years. Whereas your college classmates will often be your lifetime friends, your law school classmates will be the ones to contribute to your professional career as well as remaining friends."

Dean Joe Knight shares similar beliefs:

> "Students need to see each other as resources. The beauty of law school is not the smart people in the front of the class, but the incredibly smart people that are all around you."

Dean John Garvey believes the power of law school as a network can best be demonstrated by the claims made in discrimination lawsuits filed against them.

> "The people you meet in law school create your first professional network. The importance of this network is so dramatic that in the pre-desegregation days, the NAACP had a strategy of suing professional schools such as the University of Texas Law School. The claim was that the relationships for getting jobs and business as a lawyer were forged during the law school years and that black students were discriminated against as a result of segregated schools. I think this was true."

And for those lawyers either recently graduated or years away from the law school experience, think again about your law school circles from Chapter Three. Perhaps you may wish to revisit it in light of these comments. Are there other people from law school with whom you should reconnect?

Chapter Seven:
Networking in Your Community and the Profession

Are You Already Active in Your Community?

Many lawyers are incredibly generous with their time and energy. They routinely give back to their communities. As a wonderful by-product of their kindness, they feel more connected to the people around them. Their involvement creates a sense of belonging as well as a feeling they are part of something more important than their ability to earn a good living in an intellectually satisfying career. For those of you who are already active in your communities, feel free to skip the Trip Down Memory Lane discussion below. For those of you, however, who have a desire to connect in a deeper way within your communities and have yet to take a meaningful step in that direction, please get ready to get connected. To help inspire your efforts, learn what others have experienced from their work in the community.

Lee Miller candidly explains his role and his philosophy regarding philanthropy in the global community:

> "Many people at my firm see me as a dollars and cents kind of guy. The real truth is that at this stage of my career, I believe the most important role I can play is to encourage significant pro bono and philanthropic efforts. Law firms are at the infancy of what they provide in their pro bono programs. Modern day law firms should serve as vehicles to accomplish social change and to leverage the money they give with other established charities, legal clinics, health initiatives and foundations. We should forge relationships with other organizations that

do tremendous good that will help the work and funding proliferate. A great number of people can be deeply helped by global thinking and funding."

Other lawyers share their views on the importance of charity at the local and national levels. Debbie Berman elaborates the connection between the individual, the firm, and the community:

"When you are operating in the community, you are also serving as your firm's ambassador. I feel very lucky because I'm at a firm that encourages its lawyers to give back to the community and gives us the support and tools to be successful. I would do what I'm doing without that support, but it would be a much harder effort."

Ms. Berman further explains that giving back to the community is driven by personal, family values, not career development goals:

"My involvement with philanthropic work is driven by my values and upbringing that if you are fortunate in your life, you should be involved in the community. I am not driven by a level networking business development plan. Because of my real reason for my commitment to my community, people know I care. I believe the commitment I give my community is at the same level as I would give to my best client."

Yet, Ms. Berman acknowledges that true giving in a community can pay professional dividends:

"I have found in my community activities that many of the people have started to overlap. The more people see you in a leadership role in a variety of contexts, the more people are willing to trust you in your professional capacity."

David Brown shares Ms. Berman's orientation:

> "When I'm working in the community, my role is to work on that project. I am not there as a lawyer looking for clients. If my charitable work results in real friendships, then there is a sincere basis to ask others for their legal work."

One of the best reasons to join a community organization is to help with your own professional growth. Kara Cenar noted:

> "When I was a partner of and in management at an IP boutique law firm, I wanted a woman mentor. IP firms are not flooded with women mentors at senior levels. So I joined the National Association of Business Owners because I felt I could find a mentor there. Being active with these businesswomen helped teach me how business owners think. I was accepted by these women business owners because I did not hit them up for business. Instead, I discussed how IP could help grow and strengthen their businesses. I gave of myself. I volunteered on committees. I also agreed to meet with any of the members for no charge for the first time to help them identify issues that I or other lawyers could help them with professionally."

A Trip Down Memory Lane...
To Recharge Your Present

Think about activities and experiences in your life that created "ah ha" moments for you. Some of you will think about a wonderful teacher, others will think about a book, a movie, or a theatrical performance. Some will remember tinkering with gadgets or computers or cars, while others will remember individual or team sports—and perhaps the special coach from that time. For some, it may be a photography class, for others, an adventure at a museum. The list of possibilities is open-ended.

How can you bring this back to into your life? The following may be some examples that resonate with you:

- Serving on the board of directors of a dance company or a local theater
- Organizing a charity event for a local hospital
- Coaching Little League
- Tutoring underprivileged children
- Working in a soup kitchen
- Helping at the local law school's pro bono clinic
- Mentoring the principal of a new entrepreneurial venture
- Running for local political office

Select three or four of the best memories and conduct a bit of research to find organizations that intersect with your memories. Create a simple list:

Memory	Organization	Contact Info

If, upon reflection, you no longer are motivated to work in areas that were meaningful in the past, spend some time thinking about and researching those areas that are important to you today.

Current Area of Interest	Organization	Contact Info

Moving Forward

FIRST STEP: Call or e-mail to set up an appointment to learn more about the organization. See if there is a fit for you.

Networking in the Profession

Stephanie Scharf opines that the importance of networking in the profession is unrelated to business development:

> "Some people think that joining bar groups is simply to develop business. Often time there is no direct relationship between bar groups and business, but there are other, equally important personal and professional benefits. I've developed wonderful friends over the years, and the fact that we work on bar projects and activities together enhances our ties. Bar associations provide a network of friends who are knowledgeable about your practice and other practice settings, who can act as sounding boards for issues that come up in your practice of law and practice relationships. Bar conferences also are a great way to keep on the cutting edge of CLE."

Judge Michael Hyman believes strongly in the importance of giving back to the profession as well as the community:

> "Besides the vital legal work we perform, lawyers need to spend time on each of these seven Fs: family, friends, fellowship, faith, fitness, fun and free legal representation. That is what makes life meaningful, worthwhile and complete. You need to think about all seven relationships in networking."

Networking in the profession should be an everyday activity—after all, most lawyers spend the bulk of their days dealing with other lawyers whether they are colleagues, clients, or adversaries. Professional courtesy is a part of networking in the profession.

Faye Knowles recalls how a lost judicial opportunity turned into a professional relationship:

> "After ten years of practice, I was encouraged to apply for a bankruptcy judge opening. I lost to a talented non-bankruptcy litigator. I called her and offered my congratulations and let her know I'd be happy to talk with her about bankruptcy. We became friends over the years as a result of that call. My first invitation to speak at the National Conference of Bankruptcy Judges (a national event that draws about 4,000 judges and lawyers) was as a result of her recommendation to the speaker's committee."

Ms. Knowles' story is illustrative of the power of true networking: when you are a gracious loser and respond in a manner that is not for personal gain, amazing things can happen.

Debra Pole notes the value of networking in the profession:

"When I was on the Executive Committee of the Litigation Section of the State Bar of California, it was a very important networking opportunity as it gave me tremendous exposure. It required a ton of work to run the annual seminars—finding good presenters, attracting the audience and ensuring the everything ran smoothly. But after demonstrating my commitment to the organization, I came into contact with nationally known trial lawyers and other powerful and well-connected people that I would never have otherwise met. Exposure means that others with business will notice you."

Judge Michael Hyman agrees with Ms. Pole's assessment of the opportunities that bar leadership offers:

"Being President of the Chicago Bar Association opened opportunities that would otherwise not have been available to me. I met and worked with Chicago business leaders, prominent lawyers, judges, incoming lawyers, government officials and the list goes on. More importantly, it gave me a platform to express my opinions on legal and professional issues of the day."

Chapter Eight:
Networking for Business Development

"You miss 100% of the shots you don't take."
—Hockey great Wayne Gretzky

Business Development vs. Networking

Business development for lawyers is a complex subject. For lawyers inside firms, it involves a mix of many things including:

- The firm's platform
- The lawyer's practice group's depth, expertise, "products" and reputation
- The competence of the firm's marketing department
- The scarcity or abundance of competitors and potential clients
- The relative demand for the lawyer's practice area (e.g. environmental vs. intellectual property)
- The "buzz" on the firm's client relations
- The individual attorney's personal expertise and reputation

These subjects are well beyond the scope of this workbook. That said, networking can and should play a vital role in helping with a lawyer's business development. We will explore that relationship in this chapter.

The Long-Term Proposition

Most lawyers who fail to develop business do not fail because they are unable to make relationships or to provide quality work. They, like all others in sales (yes, lawyers *are* in the business of selling legal services), need to do the one thing that they hate: ask for business and close the deal. Business development *does* require asking for business and closing the deal. Networking is *not* about asking for business or closing the deal. Networking is the mechanism for positioning a lawyer to get business, over time, based on his or her relationships.

Stephen Ball observes:

> "It's about the relationship, not the transaction."

Joan Lebow comments on her shifts between private and in-house practice and the long-term nature of networking:

> "In my twenty plus years of practice, I have alternated between a private firm, a position as a general counsel for two companies and now am back in private practice having founded a law firm. For four of those years I was in both worlds at the same time, working as general counsel and in my practice. I have learned that you will always be disappointed if you network opportunistically for a short-term or self-centered purpose. When it is about *you*, it is so transparent it is painful."

Mr. Ball concurs:

> "Life is a marathon, not a sprint."

Unlike closing a business deal, networking is a handshake commencing an on-going relationship.

A True Story

A close friend started his career, as do most lawyers, with a firm. After a number of years, and some lucky breaks, he received a fabulous offer to move in-house. Not unlike friends you know, there was a change in management at his company and his once secure and prestigious job was at risk. While he had been in the general counsel role, he had been heavily involved in developing his law firm panel and became very close friends with a number of heavy-hitters at the major firms. Then, an incredible offer came his way: he was invited to open the New York office for a leading global firm. The temptation was too good to resist, and, with his current job at risk, he accepted. Suddenly, he found that— with two exceptions—all his old and dear friends (the ones to whom he had been handing out legal work when he was general counsel) were no longer returning his calls as promptly, if at all; he was now their "enemy" competing for the very work and clients they sought. The exceptions were two partners from different, but equally prominent firms. Fast forward several years later and my friend was once again approached with a wonderful opportunity to return to another general counsel role. Once again, he had literally millions of dollars of legal work that would be spent on outside counsel.

You know the ending. He tapped the two lawyers who had maintained cordial relations, making their firms the first to receive his outside legal spend. For one of the firms, the engagement was the largest single-client engagement ever received.

And the moral of this story? Life is cyclical. What goes around, comes around. People who are one day your subordinates may the next day become your supervisors or potential clients. Courtesy and respect must be genuinely demonstrated to the *person*, not to the *position*.

Case Study

One of the people you trust the most to share your business development fears is your husband. He's constantly reassuring about your great personality (he married you after all), your brains, and the great firm where you work. That only makes you feel more anxious. He, unlike you, just seems to breeze through every business encounter. Fresh out of college, he rose quickly in his company to brand manager and his boss has recently hinted about a promotion to an even broader marketing position. Men and women alike seem to gravitate to him, his stories, and his ease of connection. He's about to go to Las Vegas for a big trade show where he'll be interacting with numerous executives at a variety of high-end companies—many of whom would be ripe business targets for you. He offers to take your business cards and "sell" you to his contacts. You freeze. What now?

- Do you tell him that only a lawyer can sell legal services and under no circumstances do you want him handing out your card like a flyer at a discount store?
- Do you thank him for his kindness and tell him that you simply want him to focus on his own company and networking opportunities?
- Do you thank him, give him a stack of cards, and say, "Please, please, get me clients—however you do it?"

Your answer and why:

_____

_____

_____

First, let me tell you that this is no hypothetical. One of my clients called me for advice about this situation and was deeply concerned about the proper way to behave.

That said, having used this as a hypothetical at various seminars, I am no longer surprised by the intense and different reactions lawyers have to this situation. Many lawyers feel that any promotion of legal services by a non-lawyer is categorically improper and to them, a husband handing out his wife's business card qualifies as a form of improper advertising.[6] Others have reacted to the marital content of the situation, strongly objecting to commingling of professional and personal lives. Yet, many lawyers have laughed at the story and responded, "If my spouse could do all my business development for me, I'd be thrilled."

So, is there a right answer? As in any interpersonal dynamic, the answer is dependent on the actual circumstances encountered. I recommended to the client that she allow her husband to carry a few of her cards (five at a maximum) with him to the trade show. She cautioned her husband NOT to go around talking about his fabulous and brainy lawyer wife but rather, if asked about his spouse, to describe her as a lawyer, working in X city with Y firm with an expertise in Z. And to stop there. He was not to "sell" her services in any manner, other than to describe her the way any spouse would tell another person about his or her spouse's line of work. But, if someone were then to express interest in her work, the husband was at liberty to go into his wallet and pull out one of her cards and hand it to the person saying, "I always carry one of her cards with me just in case someone needs to connect with her." The wife also admonished her husband to spend the bulk of his time, energy and effort working on his company's products, suppliers, customers and prospects. One exception was suggested: if during the course of the conference, the husband heard people asking people if they could recommend a lawyer in their hometown, he should jump at the opportunity to promote his wife!

---

[6] This insight should be read in the context of the jurisdiction in which you practice and its rules and regulations regarding lawyers' advertising.

Another True Story

Lee Miller tells a story about a leading lawyer with whom he worked over several decades. The names have been changed for privacy.

One of the firm partners, Mark, had a tailor, Sam. The tailor had a client, Barry, who needed a lawyer. Sam recommended Mark. Mark, in turn, recommended Joel, one of his partners that specialized in the area Barry needed. Barry hired Joel who did such a terrific job that the party on the other side of the deal, Steve, hired Joel for his next deal. That next deal was a complex joint venture involving a Fortune 500 company headed by Fred. Fred was so impressed by Joel's representation of Steve that Fred hired Joel for his company's next significant transaction. Over thirty years, major companies continue to hire Joel and let go of their long-standing counsel.

Per Lee Miller:

> "Part of being a great lawyer is obviously substantive legal ability, but the often forgotten part is the need to cultivate and maintain relationships. Joel made an effort to spend time with the top and mid-level executives for the companies he represented and worked with them personally to 'get into their heads.' As these executives moved to different companies or rose in their current companies, Joel stayed in close contact with them, serving both as their friend and their lawyer. These executives promoted Joel to their business affiliates because of the kinship they felt with Joel and because of the respect they had for Joel's legal ability."

The moral of the story? Lee Miller believes that:

> "Networking doesn't get you business. Being a great lawyer gets you business. The relationships you develop while being a great lawyer is what networking is all about. New lawyers must focus on honing their technical skills and becoming the best lawyers they can be. The rest will follow."

Lee Miller is not alone in this thinking. David Brown agrees:

> "Networking is useless unless you are a good lawyer… and you are capable of doing a good job for the client. Most work comes from existing, happy clients. If they're not happy, they won't give you additional work or make any referrals."

Current clients are often the best source of new business—either though additional work to you or other members of your firm or through referrals to their peers. What if three of your current clients said to you, "How can I help you?" How would you respond? Can you list three current clients who you would be comfortable asking for additional work or referrals without them first asking you how they could help you? Be specific in what you seek—such as, "Can you introduce me to X at Y company?"

Current Client	Request

Common Networking Mistakes

Among the biggest mistakes lawyers make is thinking hierarchically. Per Debra Pole:

> "Once a partner from a former firm chastised me by asking, 'Why are you talking to this person? He is a nobody.' I thought then how foolish the partner was. Everyone is a somebody. Everyone should be treated with respect. You never know what person will rise in an organization and who will be terminated and who will control the business. It is important to be respectful and to get along with everyone. Many lawyers carry a foolish arrogance about what they do and who are their contacts."

Another mistake lawyers make is pre-judging the value of a potential connection. Stephanie Scharf notes:

> "I think you should network with anyone who comes in your path. People often have preconceptions about who would be good for their networks. But people can surprise you with an enormous benefits including referrals, creative ideas, and information. If you have preconceived notions then you are greatly limiting the benefit of a network."

FOOD FOR THOUGHT: Great business referrals come from lawyers who are conflicted out of the litigation or transaction. Those lawyers also are your competition. Your competition can become a tremendous business asset depending on how effectively you network with them.

Chapter Nine:
Networking for Your Next Job

General Networking vs. Networking for a Job

Networking generally offers lawyers the chance to meet new people, learn new ideas, connect with new organizations, and otherwise expand their horizons. When networking for a job, you need to be more focused. While the same rules of courtesy and mutuality apply, it is quite appropriate to tell the person with whom you are networking that the impetus for the outreach is to help you find a job.

HINT: If you have been an active networker when NOT seeking a new job, you will find it far easier to connect with a variety of people than if you first start networking when in a job search. Marla Persky artfully expresses this concept:

> "The key to networking is doing it when you don't have to. When you network out of need, but have not first built out the chits on the front end, all you are is someone else with his hand out."

Kathy Morris and Jill Eckert McCall have written an excellent chapter on networking in the ABA publication, *Direct Examination ... A Workbook for Lawyer Career Satisfaction.* Among their pearls of wisdom, they suggest a high level of preparation preceding a networking call. These guidelines are particularly helpful when the call is for a job search:

- Set goals for each phone call
- Plan what you will say
- Practice what you intend to say
- Anticipate the conversation
- Be considerate of busy people's time

- Stay organized and take good notes
- Use care to protect confidentiality constraints
- Motivate others to help you

In their networking chapter, the authors give further advice on leaving voice-mail after several unsuccessful attempts at reaching a contact. They recommend your message be something like this:

"I'm _____, and am calling (choose one)

- At the suggestion of _____
- As a fellow alum of _____
- Because I saw you give a talk on _____ at _____

I wanted to touch base with you briefly so if you could give me a quick call at _____(#), I would appreciate it. Thanks so much."

When It's Networking and When It's an Interview and How to Tell the Difference

Whether you are answering a newspaper advertisement, responding to a website listing, calling a headhunter, or replying to a company posting, you are engaged in a traditional job search. If your resume and cover letter warrant, you will be invited in for a job interview. The job interview may be conducted by a variety of people inside and outside the hiring organization. Sometimes a human resource specialist or recruiter will screen you, while other times you will be interviewed directly by the person to whom you would report. Without regard to where your interviewer sits on the ladder relative to the hiring authority for the position being filled, you are in a formal interview situation.

Beyond reviewing resources linked from the ABA Career Counsel website, http://www.abanet.org/careercounsel, visit the local bookstore to find materials on preparing for interviews, including how to dress; writing effective cover letters and resumes; and asking the right questions, including the delicate ones regarding salary and benefits.

Networking is *not* an interview. When you are in networking mode you must not confuse it with being in interviewing mode.

Interviewing Mode	Networking Mode
You are applying for a specific job. You are selling yourself for this position. In addition to asking about the company and job expectations, you will be demonstrating how your skills, expertise, training, and personality are the right match for this position.	You are asking someone for advice and possible referrals to help you move into your next, unspecified, professional job. You are learning about this person's company and his or her professional responsibilities. Depending on the intimacy of the connection (an old friend or someone you have never met before) you are having this conversation on the phone, in that person's office (for under one-half hour), or grabbing a quick cup of coffee or lunch.
Not unlike looking for business from a prospect, you must ask for the job and try to close the deal!	Under **only one** circumstance can you ask for a job: When that person says to you, "It turns out we're looking for someone with your exact qualifications. Can you interview with us today?"

QUESTION: In addition to asking about your networking contact's company and job, what else should you ask? Why?

_____

_____

_____

Remember that networking is mutual and reciprocal. Even when the other person has graciously agreed to talk with you about your job search and all parties know the focus is on advice in this area, you are not excused from acting in a reciprocal manner. Always find a point of commonality during your discussions. And try to find some way you will be able to thank this person for his or her time—such as by sending a relevant article on a topic you discussed.

QUESTION: Why are you not allowed to ask for a job when you are networking with someone who seems to be in an organization that would be a perfect fit for you?

_____

_____

_____

This is a very delicate and sometimes painful situation. As you learn more and more about your contact's organization, it may become obvious that you really want to work there. And you're just about to jump out of your skin and ask if they have a job for you. Here's why you can't do that: the person with whom you are meeting is presumably learning about you, your background, expertise and types of opportunities you are seeking. That person is undoubtedly aware of your interest in his company. You can ask, toward the end of the meeting, whether there are other people inside or outside of his organization with whom he recommends you speak.

Networking While Currently in a Job

Networking while working can be a tricky maneuver. Few people have the economic freedom (not to mention health care coverage) to stop working and then systematically look for their next job. Yet, just the act of looking for a job can jeopardize one's current job if word gets out about your inquiries.

What to do? Be wise in making networking connections. Be sure only to call upon names given to you by people you trust. Make sure that anyone with whom you discuss this matter knows that it is highly confidential and that you have not told your firm or company that you are considering leaving.

Otherwise, the nuts and bolts of networking covered in earlier chapters are true here as well. When you call people, make sure to listen to them twice as much as you talk. Remember to ask for safe leads. In some instances, you can ask that person to talk to the leads about you—not by name or firm, but by generalities and qualifications to see if it would make sense for you to contact a lead.

QUESTION: Where should you start networking?

_____

_____

_____

HINT #1:   Remember your 12 circles in Chapter Three? That's the base from which your job search should start.

OBSERVATION: Keeping your current network truly current is the best way to facilitate a quick leap into the job search process.

QUESTION: What else can you do?

_____

_____

_____

HINT #2:   One of the best ways to get a new job is by being highly visible in your current job.

- Have you been active in professional associations as a speaker or writer?
- Are you considered an expert in your field?
- Have you received press coverage for any of your deals or management initiatives?

If the answer is "no" to all of these, perhaps it is time to consider raising your profile to make your job search more fruitful!

Networking While in Transition

Even if you've been let go due to a change in management (e.g., new CEO putting her own general counsel in place) or downsizing, merger or divestiture, or even disbanding of a firm, "in transition" usually carries a silent message: "I have been fired from my job." As a result, many people feel frozen. This need not be your reaction.

If you are currently in transition, you should feel free and open to a world of possibilities. You are not bound by any of the cloak and dagger games that people sometimes play when they switch jobs while working.

HINT: I recently met a woman at a professional association meeting. Immediately below her name on her nametag she had written, "In transition." I thought this woman was simply brilliant. First, she didn't have to go through the painful response to everyone's initial question, "Where do you work?" and have to explain the details of where she used to work and why she was no longer there. Instead, when people approached her, they were more tempted to ask, "What kind of job are you looking for?," opening up a very positive and helpful conversation.

This is an opportune time to look at your career options critically. Before you leap into the first job that is offered, make sure to determine what job you are really seeking. Networking is a terrific way to learn about a whole range of options:

- Pursuing job opportunities in new cities
- Moving in-house from a firm
- Transitioning back to a firm from in-house
- Stepping into a government role
- Moving to a non-profit
- Taking on an alternative career such as teaching, writing, or consulting
- Exploring entrepreneurial business opportunities

In Chapter Ten you will be learn about creating databases and the importance of follow-up in the networking process generally. When you are networking for a new job, you may want to have a specific chart to help you keep track of all the connections you make. The chart below is an example only. You will need to design one that works best for you.

Job Search Chart

Date	Contact Title & Address	Initial call or meeting	Comments	Initial Follow-up	Next call or meeting	Secondary Follow-up	Thank you
10.15.06	Sally Smith, GC Widget Co 12 Main St Anywhere E-mail: Cell:	Met at NAWL conference; discussed her industry, the conference speakers, and my current search. Suggested I call Fred Smith and send Sally my revised resume	High energy, wore glasses, great jewelry, three kids all under 12, husband's a doctor	Called Fred Smith and set date to meet	None scheduled	9.20.06 Sent revised resume; will reconnect on 11.15.06 to advise progress of search	9.15.06 Sent handwritten thank you note indicating I had called Fred Smith and would be sending a revised resume within the week
10.20.06	Fred Smith (contact details)	Spoke with him re: Sally Smith's suggestion to call; asked for an in-person meeting	Very gracious, thought the world of Sally Smith, indicated busy on Mondays and Fridays * * * * * In person: tall, well-dressed, office filled with pix of college sports teams and current golf trophies	Sent e-mail confirming 9.22.06 meeting	Met on 9.22.06; indicated he would think about appropriate introductions	Will reconnect with him in two weeks	9.22.06 Sent handwritten thank you note indicating that I would follow-up in two weeks

While your 12 networking circles will be helpful when considering a job search difference from practicing law, it is also important to think about meeting very different people than you already know. This can and should be fun. Go to conferences. Go to job fairs. Write away for information on executive MBA programs, coaching certification and the like. Pretend like you just graduated college and the world is at your beckoning.

Just remember that it is important not to lose sight of the need to reach a point where you tighten your search and clarify your niche. It is difficult for even the most generous of networkers to provide quality assistance if you fail to articulate what you are seeking to do.

Howard Tullman runs several businesses and chairs several boards. For those of you considering a venture into the business world, first heed his advice:

> "You will experience three rude awakenings when you leave the law. One, not everyone is a type A lunatic. Some people just want jobs and you will need to hire some of those people to build a viable company. Two, you will lose the perceived economic status of being a lawyer...Three, in negotiating with potential investors, you will need to rely upon the concept of opportunity costs in order to avoid mortgaging your future as well as your children. So, before you set out to talk to strangers about a new business, it is important to connect with as many different lawyers and clients as possible who already know your status in order to save time and successfully finance your enterprise. When practicing law, you will encounter many successful business people. These people will give you important access through introductions should you decide to enter the business world."

If you are seeking a non-legal position in a corporation, government agency, or non-profit, networking will play a key factor in your success, not a search firm. Jill Wine-Banks speaks with great experience and authority on this topic:

> "If you want to change careers, networking is the ideal tool. Search firms are not [the ideal tool] because they are not set up to help you. In general, a search firm looking for a CEO for a $2 billion dollar company looks for someone who is currently happily employed as a CEO for a $1 billion dollar company. They look for an exact match of experience, not transferable skills."

A True Story

Although this story is a little dated, occurring pre-9/11, it shows that lawyers can be creative about how they arrange to meet new people:

A highly successful in-house counsel had achieved many of his personal and career goals. He was happily married with four children. He was well regarded professionally and had always worked in industries he enjoyed and found challenging. In the course of moving upward, he made a sacrifice not unique to lawyers: he moved his family away from "home" to a new city to pursue his career. For a number of years, they were all good sports and tried to enjoy their new life. But, as the children got older, everyone wanted to return to their "real" home, where their extended family lived. The lawyer engaged in the typical job search techniques. He called friends who still worked in his hometown and he sent resumes to appropriate headhunters. After rigorous efforts, he still was unable to find an appropriate position that would match the salary, benefits and status of his current position. Then one day he had an insight for a ploy that just might work.

This is what he did:

He went to the airport daily for several weeks and struck up conversations with those headed to his hometown. You know the ending of this story, I'm sure. Yes, this strategy is what helped him find a wonderful job back in his hometown: one of the people he met introduced him to someone who introduced him to someone ...

Moral of the story? Creativity, networking and perseverance separates out job seekers from job finders.

Jot down three creative ways to position yourself to meet new people relevant to your search:

1. _____

2. _____

3. _____

Another True Story

Something about flying long distances in first class tends to make gentlemen and ladies out of most of us. A friend of mine named Jeremy was sitting in his coveted window seat at the front of the cabin. No sooner than he had pulled out his work for the long journey, did a man approach him looking to change seats. As he looked up from his journal, he saw one of the nation's most prominent and well-recognized industrialists. Politely the man asked Jeremy if he would mind switching to an aisle seat at the rear of the first class cabin so that he and his wife, who was seated next to Jeremy, could sit together. Of course, my lawyer friend obliged.

Later in the flight, Jeremy chanced to be at a drinks station with the industrialist's wife. He said hello to her, referring to her by surname, and commented that he was disappointed not to be sitting with her. She smiled and said, "Well, of course, you know my name because you saw my husband earlier." My friend did not miss a beat. He joked, "No, I've seen you grace many magazine covers." Charmed by my friend's manners, she asked her husband to join them.

My friend then engaged in a conversation with the husband. Quickly they found commonalities. Jeremy would have given his eye teeth to leave his company for a job with the industrialist's company. Instead of asking for (or even hinting about) a job or discussing the company's legal department, Jeremy asked if he or his company could do anything for this prominent man. Ironically, there was a favor this man needed for one of his children and my friend's company was potentially in a position to assist. Upon return home, my friend, calling in favors of his own, provided the requested assistance to this man's daughter.

Did you predict that my friend now works for this man's company as its general counsel? If so, you were wrong. But, why not? Did he eventually get around to talking about his interest in the company, go through the interview process and not get hired? Did he fail to alert this man about his legal career and his willingness to switch jobs? Neither of those scenarios is correct. He did ask, several meetings later, if there were opportunities at the company. He was steered to the proper contact to start a hiring process if he so desired. But he determined that he preferred his relationship with this man as a friend rather than as an employee. He felt that connection would be useful to him in the future and decided not to squander it on a mere job.

Moral of the story? Not every job that becomes potentially available should be grabbed—even if it comes through great networking relationships.

Name three situations in which you would turn down job possibilities for a shot at something bigger:

_____

_____

_____

Case Study

Sally Robinson was happily serving as chief litigation counsel for Acme Incorporated when, to her shock and dismay, the
company was brought out by Bigger and Badder, Inc. Sally
was given a decent severance package and sent packing.
Always a good networker, Sally understood that the best
chance to get a new job that was as terrific as the one at Acme
was to start contacting all of her friends, family, and colleagues to get the lowdown on the legal and business market-
place. She figured most of the good jobs never even make it
to search firms, so she was eager to be in front of any and all
opportunities. True to her reputation, Sally conducted an out-
standing networking search. She analyzed her resources and
prepared a schedule of priority contacts and diligently pur-
sued each one of them, including the referrals she obtained
from her preliminary contacts.

Sally's number one target was the Superior Corporation and
her networking contacts landed her in the office of one of its
top executives one morning. She and the business executive
had the perfect conversation—including the officer's comment that he thought Sally should be considered for the company's open position of chief litigation counsel. And then the
bombshell dropped. The search for the position was already
underway and Superior Corporation was using a search firm.
He told her to send her resume to the search firm and mention

in her cover letter that he made the suggestion. Her heart fell to the floor and she struggled to keep up her energy level as they finished the conversation. As she left Superior's offices, Sally felt that all her networking efforts to get to that conversation had been wasted; surely no recruiters would consider her a viable candidate if they had not already contacted her on their own. What should she do now?

1. Simply forget about this opportunity. It would only aggravate the recruiter if she sent a resume saying one of Superior's executives suggested she write. The company clearly will be filling the opening from the search firm's slate of candidates—if for no other reason than to justify Superior's use of a search firm.

2. Realize that this job is already lost as the search firm has begun the search, but contact the firm anyway, asking to be placed in their database for future searches for other companies.

3. E-mail a cover letter and resume referencing the connection with Superior and ask to be considered for the chief litigation counsel position, and follow up with a call/voice-mail again referencing the connection if she doesn't hear back within a week or so.

4. Call the recruiter, quickly identify the connection with Superior's executive, and very forcefully request an interview.

Your answer:

_____

_____

_____

To help sort out an intelligent response to this quandary, I spoke with Miriam Frank. She notes that under these circumstances, any good search firm would welcome an e-mail with Sally's resume and a cover letter indicating the connection with the company.

> "*Finding* candidates is a surprisingly small part of the search process. What a client is really paying us to do is to sift through the universe of potential candidates. Our job is to understand the company's culture and needs and recommend a candidate whose skills, personality and style are the right fit for the job. Sometimes that person is someone they already know, but they want us to vet them against the larger pool of candidates. Companies hire search firms to act as their intermediaries so that all candidates, whether internally or externally sourced, get equal treatment and an independent evaluation. In fact, rather than throwing out Sally's resume, because it came with a company 'endorsement' the recruiter will certainly give it careful consideration. If both the company and the search firm have identified the same individual, the evidence begins to mount that the person is a viable candidate. The more contacts and information we have about the person, the better chance that person can demonstrate that he or she is well-regarded both internally and externally and the right fit for the job."

Ms. Frank further advises that in other job searches, where you know neither people within the company or the search firm conducting the search, you should nonetheless send a letter to the search firm. You may be a perfect fit. And, even if you are not the right candidate for this job, the recruiter will put you in the related database and consider you for future searches.

And Speaking of Recruiter Relations

Many lawyers find themselves too busy, too successful, or too important to take the unsolicited call from a headhunter. This is an unfortunate attitude. Anna Richo explains a better approach:

> "First, always take the headhunter's calls. Even if you are not currently looking for a new job, be polite and make sure to give [the recruiter] names of people who may meet the requirements. When you are actively seeking a new job, recruiters will remember your courtesy."

Moreover, remember how networking can **RAISE** your profile? The ability to give someone an employment opportunity is a great gift. Veta Richardson also observes: "There is a perception of being more influential if you can introduce others." And you never know. Maybe the headhunter is calling with the perfect opportunity for you.

Networking Requests

What do you do when your phone never stops ringing from people "networking" with you for job assistance?

Helping people when they are looking for their next job is one of the greatest gifts we can give to our colleagues. Never refuse your help. If you are too busy to meet with a person, be honest and say that your schedule does not permit a get-together. But, ask the person to send you his or her resume. And when the resume arrives, do not push it aside to another part of your desk. Look at it. This will only take two minutes of your time. See if there is anyone else you know that this person should speak with. Determine if there are areas in the resume that need better description or explanation. Then send a quick e-mail to the person (everyone includes their e-mail addresses on their resumes these days) that you received the resume, had a chance to look at it, recommend they call so-and-so or that they may want to clarify something you noted. Total time spent by you: five minutes. Level of appreciation, especially if from a stranger: enormous. You will always be remembered as a thoughtful person. And, guess what? One day, shocking as this sounds to you, that person may be interviewing you for your next job.

Looking Back on Their Careers...

Many top networkers recognize that while not actively engaged in job searches, their continuous networking activities—making and keeping friendships and being active in the bar and community—resulted in jobs they received.

Marla Persky recalls:

> "My own jobs have all been as a result of networking that I didn't even realize I was doing. My entry job at Baxter was the result of a classmate calling another classmate, my friend, asking if he wanted to go in-house with one of our classmate's clients. My friend wasn't interested, but he knew the job fit perfectly with my work and my interest. Though that connection, my resume was sent to the company. I got an interview and the rest is history. My current position is the result of a headhunter calling me— seemingly out of the blue. After I accepted the offer with my company, I asked the recruiter to tell me why I was part of his candidate pool. I was a speaker at a seminar that one of his partners attended. But for the fact that I had spoken, he would not have even known of my existence."

The Honorable Judge Joan Gottschall echoes the role of networking in her career:

> "Most of my jobs were a result of networking. People who knew me, or knew of me, contacted their friends and colleagues and provided wonderful professional opportunities."

Whether you're seeking the same type of position or looking for something totally new, networking, when used properly, can serve a critical role in shortening the length of the search and in locating a terrific opportunity.

Chapter Ten
Follow-Up and Databases

Do not underestimate the critical role of follow-up and databases in the art of networking.

Throughout the book, we have talked about the need for follow-up and the concept of mapping our connections and making new contacts. Here's how:

Follow-Up

In order to follow-up properly, you need to be prepared. Here are the basics:

- Carry high-quality business cards with you at all times. I can think of only two possible exceptions to the high-quality requirement: first, if you are in a government position and second, if you work for a non-profit. Otherwise, if your firm or organization either fails to supply you with cards or provides you with flimsy ones, get your own cards printed. List your firm or organization's contact information, but always carry a card that you are pleased to give to another person. Here's why: what if you run into a truly important person who is critical to your professional success? How would you like to appear to that person? Your business card is a significant part of the impression that the person takes away about who you are.

- Include out of the office contact information where applicable. For most lawyers in private practice, clients expect to be able to reach them at all times and their cards typically include cell phone numbers and e-mail addresses to accomplish this goal.

- While talking to a new contact, ask to exchange business cards. After your discussion has ended and as soon thereafter as you can do so conveniently (in the elevator, bathroom, cab, etc.) jot down notes about key elements of your conversation. Maybe you realized you had a hobby or friend or client in common. Perhaps you swapped stories about your kids. Possibly they asked (or you offered) to connect them with someone at your office. In just a few words, write down the "connection kernels" between you. Note that some people like to also jot down information about some physical aspect of the person, e.g., jewelry or clothing worn, hairstyle, or facial features. Whatever notes you take should be help jog your memory. To this end, you should write the name of the event or occasion in which you met the person and date the card!

- Transfer your notes to a database (see below).

- If you intend to be away from your office for a day or more, make sure you put a voice-mail message on your machine with alternative contacts for you so that you (or your back-up or assistant) can be reached when someone calls. Also, set up an out-of-office message on your computer with alternative ways to reach you.

- Follow-up with a new connection within two business days of the initial meeting. If you promised to get him or her specific information, however, the follow-up must occur within one business day (unless you are at a conference or other multiple-day event, especially out of town; then the follow-up is at the conclusion of the event). The follow-up can be as basic as an e-mail saying, "Nice meeting you yesterday at the CLE conference." A more detailed follow-up would be better such as, "I enjoyed meeting you yesterday at the CLE conference. Thanks for the tip on restaurants for when I'm heading to D.C. Perhaps we can get together when I'm in town for a drink."

- Small gestures speak volumes. Do what you say you are going to do. If you tell someone you will connect them with a friend, or send them an article, or help out at a charitable event, you must do what you said you would do. If you fail to carry through with your offer, you will not be credible and that person will not include you in his or her network.

On the quality of the follow-up, Carolyn Clift has specific suggestions:

> "You need to make time to have breakfast or lunch or otherwise get to know a new person. You need to calendar an effort to stay in touch with people. It must be painless to get together and respectful of everyone's time constraints."

Michael Nemeroff offers insights on the caliber of your follow-up and the likelihood of getting business opportunities:

> "The best thing I ever learned about networking is the importance of follow-up. Most lawyers have the opportunity to do this but they often get busy and don't get to it. If you don't follow up in marketing, the potential client will assume that you won't follow up in service either. Branding only gets you in the door once. Service is the key."

- When someone does you a favor, the follow-up must be personal and immediate. My preference is a handwritten note. It need not be long or gushy, just to the point:

"Thank you very much for taking the time to meet with me yesterday to talk about opportunities in the publishing industry. As we discussed, my son is very eager to write the next Great American Novel, and your introduction to the owner of Random House is most appreciated. Please let me know if I can ever be of assistance to you in your endeavors, particularly with your new bass fishing venture."

Professor Nancy Rapoport gives practical advice:

"Early in life, my mother taught me the importance of a handwritten note. Whenever you want to congratulate or thank someone, you should take the time to write a personal note."

• Remember to include, when appropriate, that person on your holiday card list.

• Follow-up again and again and again. You need to figure out a system, appropriate to each contact, for maintaining connections. Although each person will differ, the tracking of this should be consistent. As discussed earlier, the "professional networker's rule of thumb" is three contacts within a three-month period to establish a new relationship. But remember to have a clear purpose in making each contact.

David Brown cautions on the importance of diligent follow-up, consistent with your personality and style:

"Most people miss out on networking and business opportunities because they fail to follow up. You need to be aggressive in this regard. Often I'll connect with people three to five times within a short period after we've met or reconnected. I figure that there is no harm in being aggressive—I'm not going to lose out on all the business I don't have. If someone doesn't like my approach then I'm probably not the right fit. But I believe most people are flattered by my passion, including my belief that my working for them will be helping them."

Cautionary Tale

Ray Bayley observes:

> "There is a sad fact about today's society: nine out of ten calls go unreturned. That is even when you are a potential customer. The corollary is that the more senior a person is, the more quickly and thoughtfully he or she will respond to you. In my mind, more senior people achieve success because they are more responsive."

As with marketing and business development efforts, it can be appropriate to send select promotional materials after an initial contact. Depending on the nature of the conversation, sending your bio or a firm brochure or an article in which you are quoted may be an appropriate additional follow-up or "leave behind."

Databases

By the time you have graduated from law school, your head is already filled with more information than any person should carry around. And, regrettably, as we age, our memories betray us. The older we get, the worse the betrayal. The good news: databases level the memory playing field.

The best advice for a new lawyer: Spend one day creating a database of your dreams. If your office uses software such as Outlook or LegalEase, you have a head start as those programs offer a perfect mechanism for setting up your database. Do not deceive yourself into thinking that you will always remember someone who made a significant impact upon you when you met. You will have 20 or 30 or more years of meeting people who will impress you in one form or another. Start being disciplined now when it is easy and you do not think you need it. This is a lifetime gift, both personal and professional. Over the long haul (and not the short run), great networking connections *always* lead to a great book of business.

The best advice for older lawyers, particularly those who get headaches when looking at computers: If you cannot abide figuring this out for yourself, this is what teenagers and legal assistants (more the former than the later) were created for. Paying a hotshot technology geek to develop what you want will be an excellent investment.

The best advice for lawyers who totally refuse to use computers in this process: Keep your business cards separated yearly, by event, and otherwise as appropriate. Keep lists. Create a bulletproof filing system that does not require any effort to navigate even if you don't look for information for months at a time. Enjoy being stubborn about computers.

The best advice for lawyers whose firms use mega client and business development databases: Make sure to provide your firm with the information you collect on clients and prospects and make sure to keep that current. That is not a substitution for your own database of your personal network. Sorry.

What to Track

Some people keep track of friends and relatives' birthdays. They are always on time with an e-mail, phone call, card, or delivery of flowers. Everyone likes to be remembered on his or her birthday. For close friends, colleagues, relatives, and clients, birthday greetings are a nice touch. For people more remote in your network, it can seem either insincere or intrusive. Stick with the people to whom you truly would send birthday greetings—do not create a false intimacy.

Things to keep in your database for all your contacts:

- Basic contact information: business title, company, address, phone, e-mail address, and, if offered, cell number. Never ask a casual acquaintance for home information. That crosses an invisible line.
  TIP: You can learn in this process whether the person has a preference for connecting via phone, e-mail or mail.
- All the notes you took on their business cards when you first meet them. You can continually add information as you learn more about the people you meet. Things you may want to note about people, particularly prospects include:
  - What they do (that goes well beyond a person's title or profession)
  - Who are their ideal clients or customers
  - Who are their major competitors
  - Who are their major suppliers
  TIP: It is the personal connection you make with people that cements a relationship.
- Figure out ways to cross-reference your contacts by industries or companies or by skills or other commonalities.
  TIP: Once you begin to expand your network, this cross referencing will be particularly useful for referrals and introductions.
- Create electronic beeping messages to remind you to conduct your follow-ups (and then, of course, make those follow-up contacts).

TIP: We all walk around with a bunch of invisible "sticky notes" all over ourselves. It is far better to eliminate the need to depend on our memories and just automate our follow-up.

- Maintain a holiday card list.

REMEMBER: especially if your networking contacts are kept in your general computer contacts list, not everyone in your contacts will be receiving a card. Print out and date your holiday lists so you see changes year to year.

TIP: Always make sure that anyone who sends you a holiday card receives one from you. This is common courtesy.

- Update, revise, amend and renew your database at least annually.

TIP: Even a request for verifying contact information is a "touch."

Today's Project

What's on your "to-do" list for today? Tomorrow? Next week? Next month? Next year?

For today, I recommend that you start on the road to being a focused networker. Here's how:

- Complete the exercises in this workbook
- Develop—and practice—your elevator pitch
- Calendar a time to update or create your database
- Use your Outlook (or equivalent) calendar or print out this upcoming month's schedule of meetings, court dates, lunch dates, etc.
- Populate this month's calendar with your upcoming networking activities—be ambitious and list at least one person to contact for each day, including the weekends. Remember the contacts can include internal connections and reconnecting with old friends.

- Remember to put the contacts' phone numbers next to their names so they're handy when you're ready to make the calls.
- Each morning print out a daily "call sheet"
- Make your first contact today! Then calendar your meeting. If he or she is too busy to schedule a meeting, ask when you should call again and calendar that date.
- If you do not reach the person, leave a short message asking him or her to call you. Calendar two days from today to follow-up if you have not yet heard back from this person.
- Look at upcoming seminars or other networking opportunities and calendar a date to research the event
- Remember to listen to everyone you encounter. Today. Tomorrow. And every day.

REMINDER: Listening is the key to learning about what matters to the people you meet. When you connect with people about the things that they care about, the relationship develops more quickly and more deeply.

A Final Thought

I think that Jerold Solovy sums it up best when he explains the secret of networking:

> "You must genuinely like people. You cannot fabricate relationships. They must be true."

I wish for each of you who faithfully worked your way through this workbook the joy of networking. Enjoy the fun of meeting new people, helping out others, and growing personally and professionally.

About the Author

 Susan Sneider is a recognized management expert on the legal industry. She works with law firms, legal departments, law schools, and legal vendors on all aspects of the business of the practice of law.

Susan's extensive experience includes strategic planning, including merger analysis, organizational structure, governance, business development, practice management, client relations, RFP development and responses, and compensation systems. She designs and facilitates retreats for leadership groups, law firms, corporate teams, and charitable boards. Susan is a skilled trainer who works with groups and individuals on marketing, career development, mentoring, and networking. She works with clients throughout the United States and England.

Before founding New Vistas Consulting in 2003, Susan was a management consultant at Hildebrandt International, one of the leading management consulting firms for law firms and corporate legal departments. She served as a faculty member for Hildebrandt Institute's programs on practice management and professional development.

Susan started and then headed the in-house legal function for Turtle Wax, Inc., an international manufacturing corporation, for five years preceding her consulting at Hildebrandt International. Prior to her tenure at Turtle Wax, she practiced complex civil litigation and transactional law. She has taught legal and technical writing at the graduate and undergraduate levels.

She has published and spoken extensively on all aspects of law department governance and management and on law firm marketing and practice management. Susan is one of the authors of the seminal West/American Corporate Counsel Association or ACCA (now Association of Corporate Counsel or ACC) joint four-volume treatise, *Successful Partnering Between Inside and Outside Counsel.*

She has presented before the American Bar Association (ABA) and various state and local bar associations, the National Association of Women Lawyers (NAWL), and the Association of Legal Administrators (ALA). Internationally, she has presented at the Legal Monte Carlo conferences and at the European Legal Summits in Barcelona and Rome. She has been featured in *The Lawyer's* Masterclass series in London as well at the LexisNexis UK Professional Education series of *Profitable Business Development Strategies for Law Firms.* Susan is frequently quoted and featured by industry publications such as *The National Law Journal, American Lawyer, Corporate Counsel, Inside Counsel* (formerly *Corporate Legal Times*) and *The Lawyer.*

Susan graduated Phi Beta Kappa from Brandeis University and received her J.D. from Boston College Law School. She is a member of the board of directors of the Piven Theatre Workshop, a theater company and acting school, and of Literature for All of Us, a Chicago-based literacy initiative. She is married with three children.